IN THE SHIMMERING

In the Shimmering

A COLLECTION OF PROSE & POETRY

LUW Press

Salt Lake City, Utah

IN THE SHIMMERING
a collection of prose & poetry

ISBN-13: 978-0988236714 (LUW Press)
ISBN-10: 0988236710

Book format and cover design by Mark E. Moody.

Contents

PRETTY

Emily Younker

T HE BUS TURNED and headed toward last stops in the dregs. Its
passengers represented the worst of the society. Everyone sat in
the same seats day after day. Pricilla sat by the bus driver, though it
didn't make her feel any better. The old driver had given her a sense
of comfort; this new one seemed as shady as the passengers. He was
younger than the previous driver and his short-cut dark hair didn't
hide the scars that covered his head. He never smiled and occasionally she caught him staring at her in the mirror above his seat.

Pricilla nodded to the woman getting on. This woman, called
Smiles, sat next to Pricilla. They rarely talked to one another, but
Pricilla always breathed a sigh of relief when she got on. This woman
talked to voices.

"Next stop, One-oh-five and South Town Avenue."

"Thanks, Gravelly," someone called from the back, probably Dope.

Everyone on the bus had nicknames. Hers was Pretty, probably
because she was the only female under the age of forty. There was
one more stop before the hour-long drive to the next stop. People
liked to talk, but no one liked personal information. If you knew
someone's name you could find out a lot of information about them.
Pricilla wondered, not for the first time, how many of her fellow
passengers were avoiding the law.

Smiles talked next to her, but Pricilla knew from years of experi-
ence that, unless Smiles called her directly by name, she should not
bother conversing. She looked at the empty two seats on her other
side. Two passengers had stopped coming three years ago, but she
still wondered what had happened to them.

1

One had been an elderly lady. Everyone called her Silver because of her fine, wispy hair. The other had been a young man. He was called Ghost because he always wore a gray, hooded sweatshirt, and he rarely talked and never showed his face. Every morning he was at the same stop as Silver and he helped her on. Once on the bus they sat together. Silver often fell asleep resting her head on Ghost's shoulder. He got off before she did and always hesitated at the doorway to look back at her. She would laugh and wave him on. Five minutes later, Pricilla would help Silver off the bus.

"Thank you, Pretty," Silver always said. "You and Hector are such good kids."

The bus stopped and the doors opened. They used to creak, but since the new driver started they hadn't. Pricilla had noticed other improvements. The torn seat covers being patched one by one. The floors swept. The windows cleaned once a week. She looked up at the mirror and the driver turned and looked out the open door. His straight-lined mouth curved in a frown as one person got on.

The large man was unfamiliar to Pricilla and she ducked her head, staring at the floor and waiting for the shoes to pass.

"Well, ain't this a pretty one." A hand grabbed her shoulder. "What's your name?"

Pricilla looked up in surprise and caught a whiff of alcohol on the man's breath. She swallowed, paralyzed with fear.

"That's Pretty," Smiles said.

A few other voices spoke up from the back, but Pricilla was too fixated on the face in front of her.

"Take a seat," Gravelly said, his voice even rougher than usual.

The large man plopped down in the empty seat next to her, his elbows resting on his knees.

Pricilla continued to stare at the floor as the bus jostled along. She felt the man next to her shifting. After fifteen minutes, his hand brushed her leg.

"Please," she said.

He lifted his hand and rested against the seatback, his hand on her shoulder. "Is that better?"

"Dude, he's hitting on Pretty," Dope called from the back.

Perv moved closer to her. His breath warm on her cheek.

"Don't touch me," she said and got up from her seat.

Perv reached out and grabbed her hand. "You're not supposed to stand when the bus is in motion."

The bus screeched to a stop and she toppled forward, slamming against the corner of the driver's seat. Perv still held on to her hand. She tried to tug out of his grasp.

"Let me help you find a seat," Gravelly said. He moved forward, his fist darting out and slamming into Perv's jaw. The large man slumped, slack jawed and a little dazed.

"Just give me a second to remove the trash." He grabbed Perv by the shirt and pulled him off the seat. Pricilla had never realized how tall Gravelly was. He stood a couple of inches over the pervert as he dragged the man to the door and shoved him out. The man lay in a heap on the ground. Gravelly shut the door and turned to the rest of the passengers.

"No one disrespects Pretty on this bus. Got it."

There were a few mumbles of protest.

"If you don't like my rules, tough. I'm the only bus driver who'll take this route. You follow me or you get kicked off. Now everyone get back into your seats. I have a schedule to keep."

Pricilla sat down and the bus started up again. She folded her hands in her lap and when she looked up at the mirror and caught Gravelly looking at her, she smiled. He blushed and turned back to the road. When her stop arrived, she paused by Gravelly for a moment.

"Thank you."

"My pleasure, Pretty."

"My name's Pricilla."

"I'm Hector." He stuttered and wouldn't look at her.

"I'm glad." She smiled and climbed off.

IN LOVE WITH YOU

It's like being a child again:
rejoicing in the crunch of orange leaves
beneath my feet,
laughing at whipped cream clouds
piled upon a mountain peak,
singing old familiar tunes out loud
in the shower, under my breath at work,
even on a Monday morning.

I feel like celebrating every sunrise,
saluting the sunsets,
applauding the stars
just for being where they are.
I want to dance instead of walking,
whistle or shout instead of talking,
leap and click my heels
at the mention of your name.

It's like discovering a continent,
an unmapped wonder world
where mashed potatoes taste like honey,
snowflakes bloom and apple blossoms
float and coat the ground,
where lovers ride the wings of wind
to reach the heights of joy.

I am wrapped in a velvet cloak
warmed by your caring,
sustained by breath of roses
and a gentle scent of pine.
I drink again a youth's elixir
from a golden goblet
and whisper thanks whenever I remember
the cherished vows we spoke
one bright November.

Grace Diane Jessen

PASSING THROUGH MORMON COUNTRY, 1850

Beth Shumway Moore

SOFT SWISHES OF THE PAINT BRUSH sounded loud in the early morning as the canvas came to life. A crowd gathered, awestruck at the quickness in producing rich shades of spring green, wildflowers of every hue and always the rugged mountains.

Finished, the artist signed his name with a flourish, and stared at the painting. One small boy pulled on his coat, breaking the silence.

"Hey, Mister, it looks like our country."

The murmuring crowd agreed, and in a swift movement, the man handed the oil painting to the boy.

"Be careful, son. It's wet."

Stunned, the barefoot boy grasped the painting with rough, reddened hands. "You mean it's mine, mister?"

The man smiled. "It's yours." He gathered his brushes, paints, and easel and moved on. The dust swirled with his footsteps in the dirt road while he wiped perspiration off his forehead. Smells from horses' droppings assailed his nostrils, and his nose twitched. His eyes moved constantly, searching for inspiration.

Melodious singing stopped him, but not the rugged men scattered along the road. Some worked on their outfits for the trek ahead. Others hastened their steps as they straightened the packs on their backs. A few rode horses, but most walked, leading a donkey with implements for hunting gold tied on the animal's back. All on their way to the gold fields in California.

It's Sunday, Jim thought. Brigham Young had brought his people to Salt Lake City three years before, and members of the Church of Jesus Christ of Latter-day Saints would honor the Sabbath. On closer inspection of the strange shelter that served as a church, and remembering the crowd who'd watched him paint, he knew several services would have to be held. It would be like his own Catholic masses with different times to accommodate everyone. That was the only resemblance to the stately cathedral in his native Boston.

Wooden poles marked a rectangle with a roof of boards. Branches were woven between the supports to offer shade. A beautiful place, a bowery he thought, unaware that Bowery was the Mormon name for their worship shelter.

He became aware of a voice, clear and sweet, that soared above the others. The voice reminded Jim of a yellow-haired angel statue in his home church. When the music stopped, the man stood trans-fixed. As the congregation poured into the street, Jim wondered if he could identify the singer. Ah, the lovely girl with golden hair must be the one.

But no. Her voice reached him. "Oh, Rachel, I'd give anything to sing like you."

Rachel ducked her head. "Now, Charlotte, you have your own talents."

The blonde girl should have that voice, Jim thought. Yet when he looked at Rachel he couldn't look away.

$\backsim$

Who is he? thought Rachel, her eyes riveted on the tall, fair man. The voices around her receded like the murmur of a mountain brook.

"Did you hear about the wagon full of wheat that was found on the trail yesterday?"

"My papa found two good cooking stoves."

"Mama traded bread and eggs for dresses and shoes."

"Their women probably never wanted to go to the gold fields. A woman in a shabby dress holding a baby cried while her husband traded off her rocking chair for food."

"But they're lucky they can get fresh supplies."

"Look at that man staring at us?" said Charlotte, with a change of subject. "So tall and handsome."

"Hush, Charlotte," said Amy, "I'm sure he can hear us."

The girls giggled while they stared back at Jim.

Charlotte flipped her hair and blinked her blue eyes. "He's walking toward us!" she said.

"Forget it, Charlotte," said Lucy, "He's staring at Rachel."

"Here come our mamas," whispered Amy. "They'll be angry we're standing in the road."

"I can hear them now," said Charlotte, pitching her voice low, and holding her skirt above her ankles. "Ladies don't loiter on street corners or stare at men. You should be home by now fixing dinner."

With Lucy pulling her, Rachel followed her friends.

Finally, Charlotte's words penetrated her consciousness. "Honestly, Rachel, haven't you had a man stare at you before?"

"You're jealous?" taunted Lucy.

Charlotte tossed her head, and walked faster. "Probably a prospector. They're no good."

"That's not true," protested Rachel. "A few have stayed and joined the church."

"Yes, and most left the church and the girls they married when winter ended." Charlotte's tone sounded so smug, Rachel wanted to hit her.

"It's true. Babies were left without fathers, too," sighed Lucy. "Amanda's baby looks like his father. Poor Amanda loved him so."

"But some stayed, and were sincere when they joined the church," Rachel argued, astonished at how angry she sounded.

"Not very many," said Lucy, giving Rachel a hug as they parted.

Silenced, Rachel walked up the path to her home. What they said was true, she thought, her mind refusing to forget the image of the man. Upset over her strong emotion, she trembled as she pulled the cooking pot out from the fireplace to check the stew. This is nonsense, she thought, but why did I feel such a pull toward him?

These same thoughts puzzled Jim as he walked to his camp, unable to erase the girl from his mind. He was unaware of his fellow travelers' eyes watching him until they yelled.

"Hey, Jim," yelled Boris, "We saw you staring at those Mormon beauties. Remember, it's look but don't touch."

"Huh," said another man. "I've heard there's a few you can touch."

Loud, coarse laughter followed the remark.

Boris spit tobacco juice at a lizard crawling among the sagebrush. "Hell, who wants to get the Mormons after you? I've heard they can be pretty rough if you look at their women. Where we're going there'll be plenty of easier pickings."

Jim didn't answer but gathered his belongings, hitched the oxen to his covered wagon, and tied his horse to the back "I'm staying awhile to paint. I'll join another group later in the summer."

"Must be nice to have a rich papa who wanted us to take care of you," Boris sneered.

Jim should have known Papa had hired this bunch of ne'er-do-wells to look after his only son and heir. Anger rose like bile in his throat as he guessed that his papa had probably promised a bonus to the men if his son returned safe. Uneasy, he knew they might try to kidnap him. Jim flipped the reins over his oxen and left, ignoring the men.

He passed a group of people who stood gathered around a cabin. He stopped, wondering what was going on. Shrill cries pierced the air, wailing, "No, no, no!"

Jim stood at the edge of the crowd and a little boy came to stand by him.

"Hello" he said, squinting through scraggly blonde hair. "Remember me? My mama sure likes the painting you gave me."

"Of course, I remember you. What's going on here?"

The boy shuffled his bare feet, stirring up dust until a man looked at him, frowned and said, "Stop it, Willie."

"It's awful sad, Mister," Willie said. "Sister Walker's little girl, Sadie, got kicked in the head by a horse. She died. Sister Walker stares at her, and won't let the men close the casket. She screams terrible when they try. Brother Walker says it's because they don't have any pictures of Sadie, and his wife is afraid she'll forget what her little girl looks like. She died last night and it's getting awful hot."

Jim nodded, understanding the body needed to be buried soon. "Can you take me where I can see what she looks like?"

Puzzled, Willie said, "Yeah, there's a crack between two of the logs above where she is. We can see her from there."

"Wait until I get a pad and some pencils," said Jim, hurrying back to his wagon.

The crack between the logs was wide enough that Jim could see the girl's face. He sketched quickly while Willie watched.

"I drew her with her eyes open. Does she look natural?"

Willie studied the picture intently. "She laughed a lot. Can you draw her smiling?"

In minutes Jim showed Willie the picture again. The boy beamed as he held the portrait with care. "You sure can draw, mister."

"Call me Jim. Can you take the picture to her mama?"

The boy nodded and wormed his way through the crowd. Jim watched as Willie handed the picture to the grief-stricken woman. She stared at the drawing and whispered, "Sadie, my Sadie." Finally she cried, choking on her sobs.

A heavyset, red-headed man laid his hand on his wife's shoulder. Tears slipped unnoticed down his cheeks, and his voice shook. "Can we bury her now, Ma?"

She nodded and reached to stroke her child's face. Stepping back, she watched, in silence now, clutching her picture. Each strike of the hammer made the woman flinch as if the nails pierced her flesh.

Jim climbed into his wagon. I should leave, at once, he thought, but deep down he knew he couldn't go—not yet. He'd been attracted to many women in his twenty-five years, but none had intrigued him like Rachel. How could he feel such yearning when he'd only seen her once? Yet he wouldn't be made welcome here because these people would assume he was on his way to hunt for gold. Gossip flowed like a mountain stream about stopover gold seekers spending the winters, joining the church, marrying women, and, caring little for broken lives and fatherless children, abandoned all for the gold fields in the spring.

Jim would prove his only interest was in capturing the west's beauty on canvas. And Rachel? How much does she have to do with my decision? he thought. In the meantime I've got to find shelter where I can hide till my so-called partners get out of town.

A large fort in the center of the tents and cabins caught his attention. He approached a man standing by one of the cabins. A piece of straw hung out of the man's mouth and, because he had so many missing teeth, his chin almost touched his nose as he chewed. He took off a battered hat and wiped his bald head with a shabby piece of cloth.

A smile softened his features as he asked, "Looking for someone?"

"No, I'm hunting for a place to stay for a few days," Jim answered, "I need to rest and buy feed for my horse and oxen."

"I'm Garr Lander. Come in. We have an empty room in the fort. Unhitch your wagon, and we'll find a place for your animals in the pasture over yonder."

It didn't take long to unpack. As Garr left, he said, "We're in the third room on the right. My missus will want you to join us for supper."

Jim started to protest, but Garr ignored him and left.

The rustic room with the dirt floor strewn with scattered mouse droppings made Jim wrinkle his nose and frown. The outside wall had openings near the ceiling so men could shoot at any attackers. Flies buzzed in and out the holes, adding to his distaste.

"I'd sleep outside if it weren't for Boris and his men," he muttered.

A timid knock interrupted his thoughts. A small boy stood waiting. He resembled the bedraggled urchins who begged on the streets of Boston. This boy, however, was clean.

"I'm Jake. Ma's waiting for you to come to supper."

Jim handed him a sack of flour. "Think you can handle this? Give it to your mother."

"Yes sir, and thank you, sir," said Jake, handling the sack with care. Jim followed the boy to another room in the fort.

A tattered rag rug covered the dirt floor, and wood burned in the fireplace. With so many bodies in the room it was stifling. Jake handed his mother the flour and she hugged it as if it were a baby. Tears came to her eyes, and she nodded, unable to speak.

Garr took it, and set it on a shelf by the rough looking table. "Sure thank you. Flour's been mighty scarce since the crickets got most of our crop last summer."

Sister Lander peeked at the stew in a three-legged iron pot sitting over the coals. "Please call me Hannah. We're having rabbit stew tonight, with wild onions, garlic, and sego roots. It tastes good with a bit of meat added."

She gave each child a wooden bowl full of soup and sent them outside. "Please sit down, and we'll eat in here where it's quiet."

Jim balanced on the box that served as a chair, and tried not to show the distaste he felt looking at the green stew. Surprisingly, it tasted good, or else he was hungrier than he realized.

"It's excellent," he said, noticing Sister Lander's anxious look.

Her timid smile beamed. "I'm sorry we don't have bread. I'll make biscuits with the flour you brought if you'll come by in the morning."

"No, no," he said hastily. "I want to paint."

Garr stopped eating and stared at Jim. "Are you the one who drew Sadie's picture so Sister Walker would let them bury her?"

Now I've done it, thought Jim, angry at himself. He didn't want anyone to know. Yet how could they not?

"And you gave Willie that beautiful picture," said Hannah, tears forming in her eyes.

"Will you paint pictures of my children if I wash your clothes, and fix your meals?"

"Now, Ma," said Garr, "maybe he wants to paint mountains and meadows 'stead of people."

I do, thought Jim, but he couldn't resist her plea. "Sure, I'll do it in the evenings and paint scenery during the day." He looked away from her smile of gratitude.

Jim longed to ask about Rachel, but he knew better. If these people suspected he wanted to meet any of their girls, their friendliness would vanish.

Later, as Jim tossed and turned on his hard bed, he was sure he felt mice running over him. What if a poisonous spider bit him? I should pack and leave in the night. He would forget this strange yearning for Rachel, and try to ignore how the memory of her haunted him. Yet Hannah's pleading expression tormented him. He had to draw portraits of her children for her. Looking for excuses to stay, he mocked himself; however, pencil sketches didn't take long. He'd soon be on his way. At last he slept.

Early in the morning, Jim took his painting supplies and rode out of the settlement. As he gazed upon his surroundings, he walked to a small hill overlooking the salty lake. The sun shimmered on the rippling water, reflecting the mountains. The smell of the salty water didn't take away the beauty of his surroundings. He set up his easel and once he started painting, the heat, the smell, the gnats buzzing around ceased to bother him. But thoughts of Rachel nagged at him in spite of his concentration.

After he'd painted for several hours, the sound of voices caught his attention. Several girls were digging around the sagebrush with sticks, probably hunting for the Sego roots that seemed to be a staple in their diet. Rachel stood in the midst of her friends. She looked at Jim. Their eyes locked until she looked away and started to dig furiously. Jim continued to paint, but managed to watch Rachel occasionally. Charlotte edged closer to him, making him smile. The other girls followed her until they reached him. Looking at Jim, Charlotte fluttered her eyelashes. What a bold beauty, he thought.

"How talented you are," Charlotte said. "You're the town hero because of your portrait of Sadie."

He blushed. As Rachel watched, he felt her expression told him that she understood praise made him uncomfortable.

She moved closer to him. "You make people happy."

What is the matter with me? Jim fought an urgent desire to hold her close. He set his painting by his easel, and reached for his tablet and pencils. "Spread out and keep digging. I'll sketch each of you while you work." It was a good excuse to study Rachel, he thought as he started sketching.

With delighted giggles the girls spread out and, while they worked, none of them could keep their eyes off the good-looking young man. Restless and anxious to see the drawings, each one except Rachel managed to peek over his shoulder. When he finished the sketches, he handed them to the girls. Their delighted squeals of thanks embarrassed yet pleased him.

"We've been gone too long," said Rachel, holding her picture with care.

Charlotte flipped her hair back. "We shouldn't have to account for our time."

Lucy picked up her basket. "We didn't have to until the gold seekers started coming through." She looked at Jim. "I'm sorry, I forgot you—"

Jim shook his head. "I'm not a gold seeker. Your mamas are right. Will they be angry I sketched you?"

"Of course not. They'll be pleased. Don't pay attention to Lucy. You're not like most of the men who go through," said Charlotte. "It's time we knew each other's names." She introduced each girl.

"I'm Jim Barton," he said. "I'm very pleased to meet you."

"We're having a dance inside the fort tonight," said Charlotte. "Would you like to come?"

Jim wanted Rachel to look at him, but she busied herself shaking the dirt off the Sego roots.

"I'll be there," he said.

Each of the girls looked around to wave at him. Rachel, however, did not. Jim hoped that she felt as he did, confused by the strong attraction. He sighed, feeling older than his twenty-five years. He knew she must be only fifteen or sixteen.

⤚

On the way back, Rachel didn't join in the girls' light-hearted chatter. She wanted to turn and run back to Jim. What is the matter with me? she thought. I must be going crazy.

Lucy put an arm around her waist, "I think Jim has fallen in love with you, Rachel."

Embarrassment reddened her face, and she felt faint. "No, it couldn't happen that fast. You're imagining."

"Rachel's right," said Charlotte, her tone sharp and irritated. "He hasn't decided which one he likes yet."

Amy glanced at Rachel, "I think Lucy's right. It's Rachel he likes."

Me, he likes me, Rachel thought, giddy with happiness. She had sensed that his feelings matched hers every time they looked at each other.

Charlotte stalked ahead, flipping her skirts in the dust.

At home Rachel glanced at the horseshoe above the door. Papa said a horseshoe brought luck. She reached to stroke it, so filled with excitement she felt she'd burst.

～

That night Jim stood watching people dance. The music, provided by two violins, a harmonica, and a whistle, surprised him with its harmony. How, he wondered, can these people dance with such enthusiasm and energy when they work so hard? Their bare feet didn't disturb the hard-packed dirt, and their ragged clothes didn't affect their spirits. The smell from the wood fire provided light and kept the mosquitos away. Memories of the elegant dances Jim had attended at home, with lavish clothing and plentiful food, made him feel guilty because of the poverty surrounding him. Yet somehow these people, who had so little, seemed happier, more content. How could they be? he wondered.

Garr found him and said, "Join us. This little filly, Lucy, is unattached at the moment."

This is good, thought Jim, smiling at the girl. I'm dancing because one of their own invited me, and even picked the girl.

Lucy's eyes met his with a knowing smile. "I'll get you with Rachel as soon as I can."

She kept her promise and soon Jim and Rachel were dancing. They bowed, separated, came together, joined hands, and nothing mattered except that they were together. Jim thought, how can I be so deeply in love with a girl I just met? But I am.

Neither was aware of the murmurings of other people. Their absorption in each other was so intense no one else existed for them.

When the dance ended, Rachel's parents, Brother and Sister Holmes, waited for them.

Brother Holmes cleared his throat, and said, "You're traveling through on your way to California. We're grateful the way you eased Sister Walker's grief. But Rachel's our daughter. She belongs here, and we'll thank you to leave her alone." He turned, and they walked away.

Rachel lowered her head, and faint pink covered her face as she followed her parents. Jim stared after them, heart sick. How could I have been so stupid. I should have danced with other girls, he thought.

The next morning, after a restless night, he went to Rachel's home. The smell of baking bread wafted to him. Sister Holmes answered the door, and a quick glance inside the cabin showed him she was alone.

"Sister Holmes," he said, the unfamiliar salutation choking him.

She studied him, endlessly it seemed to Jim. Finally she moved aside. "Come in. We need to talk."

"I've fallen in love with your daughter, and I could never harm her in any way," he blurted. Aghast, he stopped. He hadn't meant to say those words. How could she believe his sudden pronouncement when he could scarcely believe it himself?

"So soon?" Rachel's mother whispered. After hesitating a few moments, she said, "I believe you. Rachel's papa may not but, for some reason, I do. Rachel is out back feeding the chickens and searching for eggs. Would you like to help her?"

How could she size him up so quickly, and approve? Especially in view of the stories he'd heard about the gold seekers passing through. He knew it was painting little Sadie that had opened the door.

Jim nodded and hurried out of the cabin. He spotted Rachel peeking under some logs. She looked up and walked to meet him. He gazed at her, trembling with excitement. The struggle not to clasp her in his arms was almost more than he could endure. Slow down, he kept telling himself, slow down.

"I came to help you," he said.

She smiled, and handed him her bucket. "Have you ever gathered eggs before?"

Startled, he realized he'd never thought about hidden eggs needing to be found. Rachel laughed as if she could read his mind.

So they talked of crops, the weather, and searching for eggs. They also talked about the next dance that night—anything but their feelings for each other.

At the dance they were together the entire evening. Her papa glowered, but her mama smiled at them.

The next day Jim escorted Rachel to church, taking her hand, not caring if it caused talk. She smiled at him, and he could see his own longing reflected in her eyes.

As he sat in the Bowery, flies buzzed in and out of the open shelter, and a few bees came now and again to create a small stir. Crying babies made it difficult to hear. How offended his parents would be at such a church service. Mama would stick her nose in the air, and lift her glasses to stare at the scene. Papa would wrinkle his nose, and leave as quickly as possible. Jim moved restlessly on the hard seat, ashamed because he couldn't help comparing the elegant cathedral of his childhood and dignified priest to this impoverished group, led by a ragged but powerful speaker. Beautiful singing, with Rachel's voice soaring, made him forget his criticisms. How wasted her voice was here. She would become famous in the East. Could he entice her to return home with him?

The next month passed quickly. Jim sketched Garr's family in pencils, but he painted Rachel's papa and mama, her three sisters, and two brothers, in oils. He sensed a conspiracy to keep them from being alone. He didn't mind. He could wait. Somehow he knew once he kissed her, he'd be lost more than he was already. The anticipation of the kiss made the wait worth it.

Near the end of July, Jim met the Prophet Brigham Young. Both Brother and Sister Holmes spoke highly of Jim to the Prophet.

Rumors were the Prophet Brigham could look into your soul. Indeed Jim felt this strange preacher of a man sensed his innermost feelings, understanding his doubts that he could ever live here. Yet Brigham thanked him for helping Sadie's mama in her grief, but never said anything about welcoming him. The Prophet had to be cautious, and Jim understood, not wanting to think anything else of the rather cold greeting. Brigham shook his hand, and narrowed his eyes as if to look into his heart.

"Be sure this life is for you before you make a decision. Then stick to it," he said, and pointed at the door.

Jim nodded, agreeing with Brigham, who had said a lot in a few words.

He had missed the first monthly testimony meeting. Rachel's excitement as they walked to the Bowery the next month filled him with curiosity.

"When you hear the testimonies Jim, you'll understand." She glanced at him, and quickly away while her hand gripped his tightly.

"Maybe you'll want to join the Church."

The longing in her voice caused tears to spring to Jim's eyes that he blinked away, not wanting her to see. I don't think I can, he thought, and felt as if something broke inside him.

Once they were seated in the chapel, the earnest, sincere voices of the speakers bearing their testimonies while tears rolled down their cheeks, embarrassed Jim. No mention was made of the obvious poverty, only thankfulness for their many blessings. It bothered him how these people could get up and tell their innermost thoughts.

An English couple stood to tell their story. Their seven children had died on the way to Salt Lake City. The mother held a baby and thanked God for giving her another child.

Impossible, Jim thought, surprised at the anger he felt. That couple is thankful for their one child. Where was their God when their seven children died? He watched Rachel as she listened with rapt attention, tears flooding her eyes. Jim felt as if a tight band held his heart. This isn't for me, he thought, grasping Rachel's hand as if he were drowning. She put her other hand over his, and held tightly, thinking he shared her emotion. Should I take her away with me? Jim thought in desperation.

Unbidden memories of his imperious parents and friends filled his mind. Jim knew he could convince innocent, trusting Rachel to go east with him, but he knew she'd wither away like a delicate wild flower. Her Church wasn't just a religion. It was a way of life. Maybe he should let her chose, but he knew it would be wrong to give her that choice. He had promised her mother he would never hurt her, believing that he never could. He also knew her suffering would be greater than his.

After the closing prayer, Rachel put her hand in his with complete trust. "It's over, Jim,"

Misunderstanding her, the words hit him like a lightning bolt. He stared at her. The adoration he saw cut him deeply. She couldn't know how her words matched his feelings. The meeting had cemented his resolve that he had to leave.

Together they followed her parents to the customary Sunday dinner. No one asked him what he thought about the meeting. It was obvious her parents felt confident his conversion was imminent. What a hypocrite I am, he thought as he gazed at Rachel.

Later, alone in his room, Jim wanted to destroy something to escape his anguish. Destroy, he thought, gathering the paintings of her family. He held a knife, ready to slash them to shreds. Rachel's eyes, looking at him from the painting, stopped him. Dropping to his knees, he sobbed, amazed at the depth of his anguish.

Late that night he packed his wagon. He'd go home where he belonged, and forget this episode in his life. A still small voice said, *no, no you won't,* but he stifled it. No longer did he want to paint the west, or ever hear any mention of it ever again.

There'd be wagon trains returning to civilization with their ruined dreams, which he could join. As he left, he stopped to lean the family paintings in front of Rachel's cabin. I never even kissed her. I thought we would have a lifetime. Why didn't I realize at once that I couldn't live this life, and that my world would destroy her? It's for love of her that I go. Will she ever forgive me? No, he thought, she would feel I've betrayed her, and I have. He closed his mind to the knowledge that her anguish would be worse than his because she was capable of love more than he was. What kind of man was he? These people had trusted him because of a few paintings, and he'd betrayed them. He stood for long minutes, unable to move, overwhelmed with sadness. His horse whinnied. Fearful of waking someone, Jim knew he must hurry.

Brigham had known, and deep anger, really against himself, filled him at the thought. So he tried to force himself to concentrate on the privileged life he'd chosen, but his mind resisted, fighting to keep hold of Rachel. It took every ounce of strength he possessed to leave her. But leave he must. After tying his horse to his wagon, he climbed onto the seat and snapped the reins over the plodding oxen.

He didn't dare look back.

SUMMER LOVE

The ragweed colored day
blossoms silvery green.
I high-step through tasseled grass
keeping up with my beau.

My left leg complains—
my knee my current critic.
My heart sings, *Follow this muscled guy…*
who invited me to picnic lunch.

We skirt the fringe of woods
heading for the river's music,
the current hurling itself over boulders—
a loud sustained song.

We spread doubled sheets for thickness
laying out our ferried feast.
As we feed each other fleshy grapes and turkey rolls,
I dream of dinner under a full moon.

⌒*Marie Tollstrup*

STAGE TWO

Chadd VanZanten

Yᴏᴜ ɢᴏ ᴛʜʀᴏᴜɢʜ ᴛʜʀᴇᴇ sᴛᴀɢᴇs when you start a new job. Stage One is when you're invisible. Nobody's sure if getting to know you will be worth the effort, and in my case they're probably right. I'm short, kind of pale, zits. That's the worst thing—almost twenty-five and I still get zits. Lots of them.

Also, I'm shy.

Worse than shy, if you ask my mom. I'm what she calls "backwards."

"He's okay," she used to say when I'd start crying for no good reason when company came over, "he's just backwards."

Stage Two is when you get noticed. Maybe you're doing a good job. Maybe you're really lazy but you're funny or good looking. In Stage Two you get invited to the reindeer games, if you want to put it that way. You can ask what someone thought of a new movie and then you go to lunch together. I've only been to Stage Two a few times because I'm not good looking or funny.

Also, I don't do a very good job.

My dad used to say, "Son, you've got a problem with your eyesight: you can't picture yourself working too hard."

It's not my fault I get stuck in Stage One a lot. Not all my fault, I should say. The stage system was designed to keep people like me in Stage One. At other jobs I've actually been demoted from Stage Two back into Stage One.

"He's just not ready," they tell each other. "He's just not Stage Two material."

I usually quit when that happens.

Stage Three is when you are one of the people the Stage Ones are trying to impress. Stage Threes decide who's in what stage. They run the reindeer games. If a Stage Three invites you outside for a smoke, that's it: you're promoted to Stage Two. I have never been to Stage Three, obviously. Even back in college when I was making lopsided snowcones at the Super Snow, I somehow let a bunch of sixteen-year-old girls keep me in Stage One for a whole summer.

Now I'm in the programming division at Barr-Kane, a little code farm in the business park over by the airport. I spent three months Stage One at Barr-Kane. That's too long—see, the longer you're in Stage One, the harder it is to get out. And you've got to get out. You can't just stay in Stage One forever. Trust me on this one.

It's not just about having friends to go to lunch with, it's about mental survival. Imagine a job where no one says ten words to you all week. Imagine having no one to back you up if you get blamed for something you didn't do. That's Stage One. You can stay there for a couple weeks, or maybe a couple months, but if I didn't make it out soon, I was gonna have to quit. Move back home, maybe.

There were at least a couple people in my department who could help me. First, there was Dimitri. He's a celebrity. Stage Three all the way. He started working at Barr-Kane only seven weeks before me, but he's just so good looking. Olive skin, curly black hair, and funny. He is so funny. Dimitri has this cat named Devastator, and he's always telling stories about how the cat can fight off dogs and take a shit in the toilet. He didn't even teach it, either. The cat just watched him and figured it out, I guess.

Dimitri is nice to everyone, even me. Smart, too. He once told me that if you eat thirty-two ounces of yogurt while you're drunk, it will sober you up. Something about how the fat molecules absorb alcohol. It can't be fat-free yogurt, obviously. So, I went and got a tub of yogurt and a fifth of vodka and tried it. Didn't really work that good—threw up all over my couch. But I did feel better after that. That's the kind of guy Dimitri is. I had seen him put people in Stage Two just by remembering their names or laughing at what they said. If Dimitri laughs at your joke, that's it: you're in Stage Two. The problem was that he always had a crowd of people around him, which made him hard to get close to.

The other person was Holly, the assistant operations manager. I figured maybe she might help me, but she was what my dad would describe as "AB." All Business. She was pretty, but she was in Stage Three because she worked hard and she was always fair. It didn't matter if you had zits (which I have) or oily hair (which I also have), as long as you worked hard (which I could maybe fake) she would treat you fair.

I figured my best ticket to Stage Two was Dimitri, but it turns out that was going nowhere. So, I started working on Holly. She always ate lunch in the breakroom at one o'clock, so that's what I started doing. I don't think she noticed. I tried to camouflage myself by bringing really different things to eat every day. I figured if I brought Cup Noodles every time, she'd catch on. Cup Noodles have a very distinct smell. It was real complicated—I wanted her to notice me, but I didn't want her to notice-notice, so I'd bring leftovers one day, then I'd bring a Hot Pocket, then switch it up with some fast food, then back to Hot Pockets. Sometimes I'd sit far away, other times closer. I kept track of everything in an Excel spreadsheet so that I didn't inadvertently fall into any patterns.

Also, I tried bumping into Holly in the stockroom. If I saw her go in there, I'd wait a few seconds and then go in and get a CD-R or some paperclips. She may have gotten a little suspicious about that. It's a small room, and I caught her glaring at me a couple times. Then again, I got so many CD-Rs she must've thought I was backing up the whole network 700 megabytes at a time. My whole desk was just blank CD-Rs and paperclips.

One day I saw Holly go in the stockroom with a big stack of stuff to copy. That's where the copier is, in the stockroom. So, I waited a little while and followed her in, and when I got there the copier was beeping. It was perfect.

I said, "You want me to fix that?"

She said, "Go right ahead."

Turns out it was an easy fix—the stupid collating unit. If you want to make double-sided copies on the stockroom copier, never use the collating unit or it'll jam. I'd only been there for three months and I knew that. And she could have fixed it. A monkey could've—there's a little screen that shows pictures of what to do. I figure she let me do it because, you know, I was there—let the peon do it. I maybe saved her from getting a little toner on her clothes, but it was really just a minor favor, and she wouldn't promote me on a favor. So, I figured I'd try to just chat with her a little, which might open a door later on. You never know.

But Holly kept her headphones in. Bad sign. She didn't take out even one headphone, and I figured if I talked too much, she might play that headphone trump card—point to her headphones and shake her head, which is the universal sign for, "I don't need to talk to you because you're a fat little loser and you're still in Stage One. Also, you have zits."

This has happened to me before. It's one of the most humiliating experiences ever, and my life is really just one humiliating thing after another, so it's not like I don't know humiliating. I do.

Like that girl on the bus last winter—she was wearing a T-shirt with the name of a band I like, and without thinking I went over and said, "Stereolab. Right on." She pointed to her headphones and shook her head with a little sneer. I wanted to evaporate. I wanted to kill her on the spot. I got off the bus at the next stop and I didn't make it back to work and I got fired from that job. They didn't even take me aside and say, "Rick, listen, this isn't working out." The guy fired me right there in front of the receptionist and everyone else as I walked in the door the next morning. But the thing that stuck with me, the thing I remember, is the girl on the bus and her little sneer.

So, Holly kept her headphones in. She was bobbing her head and pretending to read the papers she was waiting to copy. The copier was fixed, but I was still pretending to work on it, opening all the little hatches and watching Holly for an opening of some kind.

She looked up and said, "How's it coming?"

"Oh, it's just about there," I said, and that was the opening. Before she looked away I said, "What are you listening to?"

She furrowed her brow like she couldn't hear me. She was getting ready to make the little sneer, the little headshake. I just knew it. I considered aborting, but I was going to quit anyway if things didn't get better, so I said it again, louder.

"What are you listening to?"

She said she was listening to Yo La Tengo. I got up from the printer.

"Yo La Tengo?" I said. "No way. They're my third favorite band right now. They're playing at Spooky's in a couple weeks. Did you know that?"

Without realizing it I had walked right up to her, within one foot. I was practically talking down her throat, and she was not okay with it. Personal space—I'm not good at that. I ran back to the printer and closed it up.

"All fixed," I said.

Here's my big mistake—I figure if two people have the same taste in music, it's at least a basis for friendship. Turns out that's just not true. I never learn.

The girl on the bus in the Stereolab T-shirt looked right through me, like I was transparent. I pointed to her T-shirt, trying to show we had a connection. I assumed by wearing the T-shirt she owed a fellow fan some minimal level of respect, but she only saw that I was pointing at her boobs. She rolled her eyes and moved as far away as possible. She got off at the next stop. I did, too, and she didn't even notice.

Holly at least thanked me, so I tried to salvage something while she made her copies.

"So, are you really into Yo La Tengo?" I asked.

She didn't look up, didn't say a word. It was like she was mentally willing the machine to go faster than sixty-four copies per minute.

"Because I have an extra ticket to the show." A lie.

"Really," she said. She didn't ask, "Really?" She just said the word, "really."

"Sure," I said. "If you want it, it's yours." Considering that I didn't even have a ticket, I should have maybe worked that a different way, but at that point I didn't care. "We could meet up at the show. Not like a date. Just an arrangement, you know, we could just meet and I'll give it to you."

"What was your name?" she asked.

"Rick."

"Rick, look, here's the 'arrangement.' I have a boyfriend and he really, really hates it when guys flirt with me at work. I've seen things get ugly. So."

Boyfriends. Girls always think boyfriends are part lover, part Secret Service, but boyfriends are usually ambivalent about beating people up. They're not attack dogs. Even the thick-necked, bouncer-type guys know about felony assault and civil litigation. Husbands, they're dangerous—brothers, too—but I have never had a problem with boyfriends.

I figured Holly was probably lying about having a boyfriend and later on I confirmed it. Turns out there were no boyfriend photos taped to the mirror on her dressing table, no aftershave or extra toothbrush in her bathroom. I didn't find any sign of a steady relationship on her laptop or phone, either. As far as I could tell, she wasn't even on birth control.

I was right about Dimitri, too. He got me out of Stage One. Finally. We got to talking about reggae one afternoon and I let him rip a couple of my CDs. When a Stage Three borrows CDs from you, that's it: you're in Stage Two.

But Dimitri kind of disappointed me at Holly's funeral. Actually, I guess it was a memorial—they never did find her. When it was his turn to speak, Dimitri said, "Holly was always nice to everyone," which is what everyone said, but no one seemed to care if it was true or not. Holly wasn't always nice, and she sure as hell wasn't nice to everyone.

Someone said the same thing about the girl in the Stereolab T-shirt at her memorial and it wasn't really true about her, either. It turns out her name was Whitney.

THE PHEASANT BY THE RAIL

I turned to refill my cup and to stand gazing out
over the deck rail across the dune grass. My eye
caught his one small movement—a lustrous green head
with ruby eye patch above neat white collar—and he
was pecking, nervously pecking, looking about,
checking in the ruffling wind for danger and eating seed
blown from the rail and put out, not for pheasants, but
for the feisty house finches to squabble over again.

I edged to the window and stood still hoping to see
close up what was not meant to be seen at all. But he
crowed his fright and skimmed low over the wavering
grass with his elegant slim tail feathers tracing the
bends of the fronds.

He'll not return, I said, and was certain—
but he did. Five more times he came creeping through
the sunglow to peck and scan, peck and scan,
leaving his clone farther out on a knoll guarding
three little grey-brown hens.

All afternoon I crouched by the window
keeping a warm and cautious vigil. Each time I'd
gently raise and adjust the camera lens and think;
This time—but that wily master of the dunes would
disappear again into his stalky domain; for all my care
and stealth, he knew I was there.

The fire in the wood stove cooled and darkness
closed over his simple path. I packed to return to the city,
reluctant, as always, but more resistant this time.
With coat tightly zipped and scarf tightly wound,
I went out to refill the feeders on the rail—then
turned back and flung the rest of the seed
along the sand at the edge of the dunes.

⌐Betty J. Vickers

TEMPEST

Tim Keller

WE POKED OUR HEADS OUT of our tents like sky-wary rodents. Greenish-black thunderheads surrounded camp. The rain was still coming, but nothing like the run-for-the-Ark deluge of the last several days. A few rays of sunshine escaped to the ground, just enough to brighten the soggy grey. Most of us went on a food run, or just stayed put, but not me. Breaks like this were rare, and I intended to take full advantage.

Some of the guys were already playing Frisbee on the parade ground. Wayne and I were slogging through ankle-deep mud to join them when the blast knocked us down. At least I think it did—maybe it was involuntary, like blinking or flinching.

There was a roaring in my ears. Exactly what the sound was, what it most closely resembled, I didn't know. The pieces of reason were slow to re-assemble.

A Frisbee was thrown—

a kid soared into the air to catch it—

there was a brilliant flash—

for a moment he was pinned to the earth like an insect in a display case. Then he collapsed and lay still, smoke rising from his body.

⌒

Wayne, me, and two guys from troop 989 get there first. The boy lies face down in the mud; a nasty red welt runs from his skull down his back. The odor of burnt hair and grilled meat permeates the air. I'm rolling him to his back when a pimply faced varsity scout grabs my arm and goes, "Don't move him!"

Wayne's ham-sized hand shoves the guy away.

"What do you wanna do asshole?" he says, "sit here while he drowns?"

Pimples turns and bolts.

Someone shouts, "Check for a pulse," but the remaining 989 kid is on it.

"None."

Wayne straddles the boy and crosses his palms across the kid's chest.

"One.—Two.—Can you do mouth-to-mouth?" he asks between compressions.

I nod and move into position.

"Three.—Four.—Five."

"Now," says 989.

I tilt the kid's head, scoop the mud from his mouth, plug his nose, and blow. The count begins again.

⤸

We cheered as our charter bus squealed to a dusty stop. Location: Moraine State Park, Pennsylvania. It could have been Beirut for all we cared; we just wanted off. Not that we were ungrateful. We'd been to Washington D.C, New York City, Niagara Falls, and points in between. It's just that after ten days the bus smelled very much like its fifty teenaged inhabitants, and I for one was ready for the outdoor portion of the adventure to begin.

We'd been drilling all summer, so camp went up fast. After that the time was ours. A service had been set up to shuttle us from place to place, but the swarm of scouts snarled traffic throughout the park. So we walked.

Sailing and swimming in the lake was a blast, but that was clear across the park. The trading post was closer, just cross the footbridge and a half mile through the woods. Plus, I had my brother's vintage patch collection, which in scout terms made me rich; not to mention popular, particularly with Wayne.

Wayne was sixteen and so big he was practically a marine. He never once complained about being stuck with a twelve-year-old;

still, I figured it was best to keep him happy.

It was day three and I'd only just finished trading an original Bridger Beaver for a Malibu Council Shark, some junk food, and a dirty magazine for Wayne, when the first dime-sized raindrops darkened the soil.

Within minutes it was pouring. Lightning struck a tree, blasting splinters into the air. A bunch of us were waiting it out under the administration tent when the announcement came over the PA ordering us back to our camps.

Steeling ourselves against the onslaught, we raced back through the woods. Only when we got to the foot bridge did we stop. Surging water, now halfway to the slats, had replaced the gentle burble of the brook.

The camp danced silver with rain. Everything was awash, then it came even harder, slamming against the canvas tents like rough music. The scoutmasters agreed, "it probably won't flood," but there was a forced quality to their reassurance.

By morning, the bridge was gone.

↜

Again the count reaches five. Wave after wave of suddenly intense wind and needle-sharp rain lash against us. I wipe his face and blow. Coming up I catch his eyes. They're wide open but nothing's there. It looks like he's crying. We reach five compressions and again I blow. His body is stiff. Something, a necklace maybe, has scorched a collar around his neck culminating in an opaque teardrop of metal, a smoking brand against pink flesh. The count reaches five.

↜

In spite of the rain it was hot. Mud smears from swipes at sweat and bug bites washed down our faces and arms. For the second time in two days we helped another troop move their camp. We didn't have to move our stuff. We were lucky enough to be on higher ground, but these guys (from New Mexico, I think, or Arizona) woke up in standing water. So we hauled their water-logged tents, bags, and equipment up this slimy-assed hill while mosquitoes swarmed around us. I didn't know mosquitoes came out in the rain, but these sure did. Sometimes they flew straight for our mouths. Kamikazes, we called them. At first we hacked and retched. After a while, we didn't much care.

Eddie had a transistor radio; between the tornado and flood warnings there were hilarious stories about "the scouts in the park"—how well we were holding up, what good care they were taking of us. Like the one about these BSA staffers who took seventy-five sleeping bags to a Laundromat in Butler to dry them.

Ha! There were 28,000 of us and the driest we'd been in three days was in the shower. Dry was a fucking memory, a rumor. Hell, dry was a myth.

Tired of digging rotting underwear out of our butts, a lot of us went naked—some under ponchos or with a shirt around the waist, some without. I didn't have hair yet, and was among the last of the holdouts. But it was impossible to keep anything clean or dry in our leaking Petri dish of a tent. My underwear and socks stank so bad I wrapped them in a plastic bag and hid them in the supply tent.

I felt pretty good about this solution until they called the assembly. Mr. Jarvis held out my jockeys and read my name off each pair.

Thanks Mom. Another muddy trip through the spanking machine.

There was plenty to laugh at, too. Like the morning the rain slowed to a mist and all these news helicopters started buzzing around like mechanical vultures. Suddenly, in came this edict from downtown: "everyone is to start wearing clothes, immediately!"

So, again we wrapped our ponchos or shirts around our waists and went commando.

Eddie's ear was glued to the radio and he looked less happy by the hour.

"Will they evacuate us?" he asked.

"Hell no." This from Scoutmaster Crandall. "This is nothing. At the world jamboree of '71, a typhoon hit and still we stayed."

"They couldn't get us out, anyway," Ben complained. "The road's washed—"

"Gentlemen," Crandall interjected, "we're here till we're not; just have to make the best of it."

The best of it wasn't so great. All the food was waterlogged, our sleeping bags were useless; they even made us stop mud-surfing down the hillsides. So, once the diversion trenches were dug, the monkey bridge was built, and the flooded campsites relocated, there was nothing to do but play Hacky Sack or Frisbee.

⤿

The world—my corner of it, anyway—is in slow motion. Someone yells above the roar in my ears, and again the count hits five, but I can't look away from his eyes! All I can think about is wiping the rain from his face.

Suddenly, I'm lifted away, and Mr. Crandall takes my place.

"Get downtown and have 'em call for an ambulance," he shouts over the storm.

Reality comes rushing back.

"B-but the road's out," I say.

"They'll send someone back with you," he says. "Now go!"

And I'm racing through the mud. By the time I reach the monkey bridge, paramedics are making their way across.

⤿

A couple hundred of us gathered to watch the paramedics work, their voices and the staccato impacts of the rain were the only sounds. An eternity went by before the words, "I've got a pulse," were spoken. We cheered like they were rock stars.

Late the next day the rain slowed, and sometime during the night it finally blew itself out. We all worked to clean up the aftermath.

Aside from "alive" there wasn't any news about the kid, not from the staffers, anyway. Eddie's radio crackled with all kinds of things. Like, there was no mention of us or our game at all.

"The storm came upon him suddenly," the announcer said, "and he was struck running for his tent."

Mutually exclusive concepts like "extremely critical but stable condition," were tossed around. The reports always ended with thoughts and prayers—the one sentiment with which everyone could agree.

The final and only assembly was attended by an amazing 28,000 scouts, plus several thousand staffers, scoutmasters, and volunteers. After the official pep talk and concert, they announced that the kid was improving—and when the cheers died down, that our thoughts and prayers were with him.

⌢

I'm trying to load a new role of film in my instamatic—but rust seals the compartment latch, and water's trickling out of the lens.

Wayne's good at fixing stuff.

I'm looking around for him when the PA system crackles "—has succumbed to his injuries. Our thoughts and prayers are with the family in this time of—"

I don't hear any more. Everyone's talking over the announcement and the roar in my ears is back. My eyes find the muddy depression where it happened, and I crouch down between some tents and hide.

⌢

Into folklore he went—neither forgotten nor remembered—the story bigger than reality ever was. Details unknown for days were suddenly gospel.

"Dude, I heard his head exploded!" said one kid.

"Not his head idiot, you don't live for three days with an exploded head, it was his foot, where the lightning went out."

Even adults got in on the act: "Vegetable," Mr. Neumann intoned. "Parents had to pull the plug."

Mr. Crandall found me as they were breaking down the tents.

"Dinnertime," he said.

"Not hungry."

"You sure? Peanut butter and jelly sandwiches, nice and mushy. "

"No thanks." I said, unable to look away from the spot.

Crandall squatted down beside me and draped his arm around my shoulders.

"Might help to talk about it."

I hesitated, if it were anybody else—but at least he'd been there, tried to save him. God, I hated the tears tickling their way down my face.

"The kid died," I said. "He died right over there, and nobody even cares."

"I don't know about that," Crandall said. "I care, I know you do; we tried, didn't we?

I nodded.

"That's the hardest part, don't you think? That we tried and it wasn't enough? Hell, the week we've had—it could have happened to any one of us."

Not trusting my voice, I nodded once more.

"Twelve years old is awful young—but you were right there, jumped in, remembered your training. I came on the run, but to see you out there, already working on him, made me straight-up proud just to know you boys, and that's a fact."

"Thanks" I whispered.

"It's the truth," he said.

"Now, there's something else you need to know, and I wish to Christ I didn't have be the one to tell you."

He waited until I looked up at him.

"How you live after something like this happens—that's what matters. Life goes on," he said. "It has to. It's cruel, but it's true. Now, you can sit there, refuse to eat, and not say a word unto anybody if you don't want to. I'm certainly not going to make you. You go on and make your peace however you need to; but you'll be home this time tomorrow. You keep this up, you'll worry your folks half to death, and I know you don't want that."

"No sir," I agreed.

Crandall stood to leave, then turned back.

"Sometimes" he said. "The best we can do is try to make it okay for the ones that care about us. You think you can remember that?"

～

My family and closest friends gather for a welcome-home picnic on the lake. In my head I'm screaming *No!* I've had all the outdoor fun I care to, but I don't say it out loud. I catch mom's eyes and I can see she's worried. Crandall must have said something. They've asked me about it a dozen times already, but I don't say much—I can't. They don't understand; he can't have a cookout, his family can't throw him a party. Still, I go along. We roast hotdogs, make root beer floats, and play games well into the night.

I hope the kid will understand.

SINGLE WHITE SOCK

A single white sock showed up in the wash today.
Its match miles away.
Separate.

A vacant chair at the head of the table.
A spot unfilled.
Bare.

One side of the bed left untouched.
Unfilled drawers.
Empty.

The future insecure.
A past redefined.
Uncertain.

He still calls me "Sweetie."
He doesn't notice.
Habit.

A life unfastened.
A focus lost.
Undone.

A single white sock.
No longer a match.
Alone.

Kendra Fowler

DRIVEN

Marilyn Richardson

IT WASN'T THE SEX. He always claimed it wasn't the sex. What was it then, power? It may be that power is all, the motivation for every act. Needing to feel control, self-validation, the ability to make things happen, prevent the bad, ensure the good, a person embraces power. Someone once said that power is a great aphrodisiac.

But he wasn't a politician or the president of anything. Not a television star or a minister with an adoring flock. He was a design engineer and highly successful at his job. Fluent and imaginative, he came up with endless new ideas and they worked. So maybe it was his inherent creative energy that drove him to infidelity.

Or perhaps it was a narcissistic plunge back into those heady teenage years when emerging hormones exploded into his system and, because his controlling personality was evident in all his activities, including religion, he had resisted temptation? Resisted and resisted and resisted, and enjoyed the added tension that resulted.

Now, as a married man, his tension came from the intrigue necessary when he didn't resist.

He'd actually been a virgin when he married. A horny, libidinous virgin. And for years he and his wife enjoyed great, lively sex. He was, during those first years, faithful, monogamous, and driven.

Then came the affairs. And his attempt to justify them.

"We have lost all intimacy," he said to his wife.

"A man needs to be coddled, treasured," he said to a coworker.

"A man needs his mate to be many things. Have you read that book that suggests woman can fill four roles, Madonna, Amazon, mother, and harlot? Wait, the term wasn't

Harlot, it was…? Anyway, I need that. I need more nurturing, more understanding, stroking, even feeding," he said to his brother.

"We never eat home-cooked meals anymore," he said to a neighbor.

"I don't mind doing my share around the house, but…" he said to his sister.

"Something is missing," he said to himself.

But it wasn't the sex.

His affair, this time around, lasted for about a year. They separated. He filed for divorce. They fought. His children were angry with him, his father disappointed. His brother propositioned his wife. His sister's daughter named her child after his wife—as though to say, she is the good one, you jerk.

He discarded his first liaison, a coworker, as being unstable, undependable, a flake. French, Charisse thrived on intrigue, lies. He hated that. He looked for someone more trustworthy, someone who would understand him, care about his past, someone like his wife.

He found a woman who adored him. Carolyn was a fine specimen. Tender, ready, eager. He found himself impotent.

He looked further.

He visited a marriage counselor. He spent hours tracing his college sweetheart (they had nearly been engaged) and phoned her long distance.

Then he called his wife. He wanted to talk, to confess, bare his soul. He wanted to be honest. She agreed to a meeting.

At the appointed hour, he rang the bell and was admitted to his own home. After subdued greetings—"How have you been?" "Fine."—came a lengthy silence. He began to circle the room, moving to his right. Across the room she, too, moved to her right. Like boxers in a ring they circled, winding up for the match.

Finally, without making eye contact, and still panther pacing, she sneered, "You bastard."

Surprised, he stopped, leaned into the empty space between them and shouted, "At least I'm honest."

"You call that honest?" she snarled. She, too, had frozen in place. Hands on the back of the sofa, head held high like a cobra, she hissed at him. "You haven't faced, yet, the enormity of your deception."

That hurt. A relationship without integrity was nothing. He always believed this; had said it often.

He tried sniveling. "You don't care."

"Don't care? Don't care?" The tendons in her neck were like steel rods, pushing her voice higher. "You bastard. You son of a bitch. Don't care? I've lived my life for you. I follow you around. I allow you the luxury of being a bumbling genius. I pick up after you. Remind you of simple necessary chores: don't forget to put gas in the car, don't forget your dentist appointment, don't forget to eat." Hot tears flooded her cheeks.

He looked away, but he wasn't through. "You care more about the house than you do me."

"You are so self-centered, so stupid. You egotistical bum. I ... I ..." She was so angry she began to sputter. Her neck was mottled, his face ashen.

He took a step away from her, then toward her, then away again, dancing his despair. He couldn't stop. With a calculated softness he said, "But you don't touch me, anymore. You don't give me any physical sign that you care. You hug the nieces and nephews, play with the babies, dote on my father. I feel jealous. Why are you warm with them; cold, walled-in, distant with me?"

He scored. She wanted, had for always, to be able to reach out and stroke his hair, the back of his neck. But she always stopped, mid-air, unable to initiate the contact.

Uncharacteristically, she started throwing things. First the sofa pillows.

"Cheat!" She turned to the bookcase. She wanted to hurt him. "Liar!" She hurled book after book at him. "You neurotic, self-indulgent bastard!" She moved to their collection of old LP's, sailing them like whirling stars, rapidly, as fast as she could pull them out, hoping one would take his head off. They crashed into lamps, windows, furniture. "Fucking asshole!"

He tried to protect himself, knock them out of the air. One hit his cheek and blood trickled down his face. "Castrating bitch!" Another hit his wrist and he was sure a bone was broken. "Selfish slut!" Pain triggered a reaction. He began throwing things, too. The air was dense with the missiles of anger. "Cold selfish bitch!"

"Traitor, blind, stupid traitor!"

Exhaustion slowed them down. Panting, she lunged toward him, swinging a dictionary, and tripped over a fallen lamp. Without thinking, he reached out to save her.

The contact, like an electric connection, welded them together. In a slow motion fall, they sank to the floor and rolled together in the fragments and shards of their cluttered battlefield, arms locked around one another, crying, laughing, embracing, consoling.

They decided to get back together.

Gradually, his life resumed its old pattern. Lively sex with his wife, poker every other Friday with the guys (when he lost, he lost big), and a new invention that brought him an invitation to an international conference. It was a prestigious honor; the company was pleased, his wife was pleased, he was pleased.

He flew to Sweden, made his presentation, and acknowledged the applause, knowing he had done well. He felt both tired and pumped as he slumped down in his chair. From the vantage of the raised speaker's stand, he scanned the audience.

A woman in the fifth row, a brunette with blue eyes and a cobalt blue suit, rose to leave. At the doorway she glanced back at the dais. Unhurriedly, she looked at each dignitary, pausing perhaps for a full five seconds on him. She turned abruptly and was gone.

He sat up, glanced at his watch, took a deep breath, and rubbed his hand over his five o'clock shadow. Would this meeting never end? Would he be able to find her? Should he slip out and follow her now? He fingered his tie, looked to his neighbor, and with studied caution, and what he imaged was a certain casual elegance, stood up and left the stage.

SOLACE

It's been a tough year for me,
Full of sorrows and pain,
Deep losses and heartache,
Long empty nights of self pity.
Then one day a sweet little voice
Came through the fog and asked,
"Can I have a sleep over, Grandma?"
Of course I couldn't say no,
What grandmother could?
The night was the same as many others
Little arms and legs all akimbo,
Little space left on the bed for me.
And then she rolled over and those
Little arms wrapped around my neck.
I still had nowhere to move,
Stuck on a slim section of bed.
But in that tiny embrace
I found an abundance of joy.
And with that soothing balm,
I slept.

Saundra Roberts

UNHOLY SABBATH

Betty J. Vickers

MID-AFTERNOON ON SUNDAY, April 16, 1928, the door of Alston Drug Store flew out of Mayor Walter Greer's hand when he stepped inside the already packed pharmacy and struggled to close the door against the driving wind and rain. For a hurricane that was supposed to be headed north *away* from Florida, this hurricane seemed to be doing its best to destroy the tiny five-month-old town of Belle Glade sitting at the southern-most tip of the shallow 730-square-mile Lake Okeechobee.

"Glad you could get here, Walt," said Charlie Riedel, the founder of Belle Glade, as he turned anxious eyes toward the mayor. "We're beginning to worry if the dike's gonna hold."

"Yeah, Mayor, what do you think?" asked Henry Martin, the owner of the Glades Mercantile Company located beside the Glades Hotel and Cafe. "Do you think she'll come through for us, or should we get our families and leave here while there's still time?"

Mayor Greer was a big man of two hundred-plus pounds with muscles developed through his trade as a blacksmith. He had an open face, a confident manner and sported a sleek handlebar moustache. He looked around the room filled with Belle Glade's unnerved farmers and merchants and singled out the two men.

"Charlie, you and Henry come with me," the mayor said. "Since we obviously can't get any official news about this 'cane with no radios and downed telephone lines, we'll go over to the Lake and check on the dike ourselves."

The three pioneers fought their way through the gusting wind and needle-sharp rain, managed to get in the mayor's Ford and drove the two miles to Chosen, Belle Glade's sister town that was little more than a settlement of related farmers grouped together. They got out of the car and struggled to the top of the seven-foot muddy dike along the Lake. Through eyes squinting against the severe squalls buffeting him, the mayor made his assessment. It was clearly a worse storm then the scanty news coming over the lines before they blew down had led the citizens of Belle Glade to believe. The mayor looked down to see the black water of Lake Okeechobee lapping a foot from the top of the dike. To his untrained eye, however, the dike looked as firm and solid as it had before the storm began to blow, so he judged that the dike would hold.

Back at the drugstore, Mayor Walt Greer informed the waiting crowd that he wasn't going to take his family and go anywhere. In fact, however, he knew it was too late for anyone to leave. To leave then would have been to risk being caught in the open Everglades headed directly into the storm, or to risk being blown off the road and into the Hillsboro canal. Every man assembled there, at least one from every family in town, understood that they would be staying in Belle Glade for the duration of the storm, no matter what was left unsaid. About 5:30 PM, most men went home in the near darkness to prepare their families.

The drugstore was located between the two hotels in town. Charlie Riedel crossed the street to the George Tedder's Glades Hotel which he had built and recently sold, so he knew it was well constructed. Henry Martin returned to his mercantile company beside the Glades Hotel and Café.

"Go get your mother and the kids and bring them here," Henry told his oldest son, Raymond. "Go fast."

By the time Raymond returned with his mother, Bessie Mae Martin, and his siblings, other families had poured into the store and were trying to make themselves comfortable to ride out the hurricane. Hot coffee brewed in the kitchen and mothers tried to calm their frightened children. Outside, the howling winds and pounding rain sounded like a dozen fully loaded freight trains bearing down on the hotel. When the lights went out, Henry and his clerk, Arlin, lit kerosene lamps and hung them from hooks in the ceiling. In the wavering eerie light and ravaging wind, nobody hear Bessie Mae's soft voice say, "Well, at least we won't starve." Little did she know that she would become one of the first victims of that unnamed hurricane.

Over at the Glades Hotel, a man and his family entered who had a working radio. He was instantly surrounded by the crowd anxious for news from West Palm Beach. The newsman was calmly stating that West Palm Beach residents could rest easy because there was no danger from the approaching hurricane. Suddenly, his voice stopped, then he screamed into the microphone.

"Oh, my God! There is a huge storm pounding the city at this very moment. Oh, my God!"

Cold terror gripped the Glades Hotel refugees. Everybody knew then they were trapped—trapped with the wind-driven waters of Lake Okeechobee already slithering over the low dike and destroying it as the water moved inland. Most remembered the monstrous hurricane that had hit two years before and killed several hundred people over in Moore Haven, the county seat. Many of the panicked hotel parents grabbed their families and ran back to their homes to take care of their livestock and pets, but stayed where they were. There was no place to go and they knew it.

The wind that had been blasting for twenty-four hours suddenly became eerily silent as the eye moved toward the Lake. Then the wind changed direction. A twelve-foot high dome formed as the water piled up on itself and careened over the quickly dissolving eight-foot high muck dike. Hundreds of people and animals living on the lake's islands were the first to drown in the killer storm surge. The storm immediately raged head-long over the farms and towns surrounding the southern end of the Lake leaving unprecedented slaughter and damage in that area known for its deadly hurricane season every year from June to November.

As the flood waters from Lake Okeechobee lapped up the steps of the Glades Hotel and rose higher on the walls of the first floor, the men worked frantically to move everything perishable to the second story along with the women and children. Terrified mothers held babies and smaller children on their laps while their older children clung to the younger. Bessie Mae was seated at the top of the stairs with her brood when the front door of the store blew inward.

A farmer, John Elliot, fell through the door as hands pulled him inside and forced the door closed.

"He's hurt!" yelled Henry Martin. "His hands are bloody!" Several men helped Elliot across the room and up the stairs so the woman could give him first aide for brutal cuts on his hands.

"My God, what happened?" asked Tempie Wells as she tore strips of cotton cloth for bandages. Annie Mae was already dabbing alcohol and then iodine on the lacerated hands.

Elliot couldn't help it. He broke down and cried as he told the women about being in Curt Johnson's house in Chosen with a crowd of other neighbors trying to avoid the raging flood.

"All of a sudden, the whole house gave a lurch, stood up on one corner and then flipped over into the canal," he said between sobs. "I guess my friends and neighbors in there with me all drowned."

Annie Mae dried his tears with a small towel. "Where was the house when you last saw it?" she asked.

Elliot pointed with a bandaged hand toward the Hotel front. "Right outside in the canal across the street stuck up against the big bridge," he answered.

Several of the women just stared at him. Raymond moved toward the stairs to call his dad. Annie Mae felt his forehead for fever.

"You can't mean right out front by *this* big bridge," Bessie Mae challenged. "Curt Johnson's house is at least a mile away in Chosen."

Elliot wiped his nose along the top of his bandaged hand. "Not anymore, it ain't" he insisted. "Go see for yourself if you don't believe me. Right outside across the street."

Henry Martin came up the steps and the women told him the story that Elliot had just described to them. Henry shook his head and smiled. Then he and the women chuckled quietly.

"No, I don't think so," said Henry. "There's just no way a house could have floated a mile down that canal with all that wind and rain out there—a barge, maybe—but not a house. He's off his head. Best put him to bed and let him rest until morning."

Before the night was over, however, more than fifty houses had followed the Johnson house and jammed up at the big bridge in

Belle Glade. Occasional cries for help that would never come could be heard in the darkness of the shrieking fury. Against all odds, the Tedder Glades Hotel was the only building left standing in Belle Glade when the storm began to dissipate around daylight on Monday morning.

The nearly two hundred people holed up across the street in the Belle Glade Hotel were not so lucky. A few were relieved when they thought the storm was finished as the eye passed over Belle Glade. Most knew it was only the 20-minute lull before the back edge of the storm would land on them with even greater menace.

As the stormed resumed and Charlie Riedel rushed the families , both black and white, up to the second floor of the Belle Glad Hotel to avoid the rising water, the roof blew off the building with a might tremble and bang. As people screamed and ran around in circles, the men braced themselves against the lakeside wall to keep it from collapsing on their families. The wind kept lifting the entire building and slamming it down again on its foundations until the concrete pilings pierced the floorboards and anchored the hotel in place.

Across the street at the mercantile store in the Glades Hotel and Café, Henry Martin, flashlight in hand, saw that the Hillsboro Canal had morphed into a murderous river as far as the eye could see. Later statistics showed it to be three miles wide. He scurried to herd the horrified families up to the second floor to avoid the water rising up the walls an inch a minute. When the water filled the second story also, Henry stood on a table, pushed open the trapdoor and shoved families into the attic. By then, the flashlight had failed and the people were in total darkness.

With everyone wedged into the attic, a huge gust of wind lifted the hotel off its foundation. It was about 8:15 PM and, although the people in the hotel did not know it, the dike around Lake Okeechobee had just disappeared under the onrush of black lake water that shot out across the entire area.

"Help, help!" screamed several women. "Were moving! Oh, God, help us," prayed Bessie Mae as she clung to her husband and children.

Unrelenting screams filled the wind as the store floated 200 yards down the street toward the Methodist Church where it crashed with a crunching blow. Water rushed under the store, turned it on its side and flipped in over on its roof. Everyone was washed out into the churning. As the store broke apart, people grabbed the broken boards and pieces of roof and clung to them. Some survived. Most did not.

Twelve-year-old Thelma Martin was tossed across the canal and into the upturned roots of a giant rubber tree where her foot lodged between the roots and held her fast. When she felt something brush her leg, she reached down into the water and dragged up her baby brother, Robert. In moments, Thelma became aware that her friend, Ernestine, and two kids from another family, Hattie and Carl, had also been thrown into the tree roots. As the flood tried to dislodge the children, they took turns holding the baby up over their heads to keep him out of the water. Before long, Hattie and her brother were swept off the roots into the swirling water and were never seen again. Ernestine, Thelma and baby brother Robert survived.

Henry Martin and his family thrashed wildly in the debris of the collision of the hotel with the church. Raymond found and grabbed two of his siblings at the same time his father lost hold of Bessie Mae's hand and she sank out of sight. Henry immediately dove to grab his wife, but a plank struck him near his eye and almost knocked him unconscious. He managed to grab a piece of roof and help his son, Sonny, up on the makeshift raft just before Raymond surfaced and crawled onto the raft with his father and brother. Henry frantically called for his wife repeatedly. Bessie Mae never answered. She was gone forever. Raymond followed his mother a short time later when he lost his grip on the slippery raft and slipped beneath the water never to surface again. Then Henry and Sonny lost their hold and were tossed into the water.

"Oh, God, please save my last son," Henry prayed as he held Sonny close to his heart. Sonny, naked where the water had stripped him of all clothing, had been seriously injured when a nail protruding from a board was thrust into his flesh just above his heart. Moments later, another board with an exposed nail drove itself into his chest just below his heart. Henry and Sonny, the only survivors of their family, were found when the water receded as they clung to the crossbars of a fifteen-foot high telephone pole on Main Street.

The faint tinges of first light shown on the eastern horizon as the aftermath of the horrendous storm settled into occasional gusts and choppy surf in the flooded streets.

Dr. William Buck, who had ridden out the storm in a tiny back bedroom with other survivors in Tedder's Hotel, made his way down to the waterlogged lobby. People with glazed eyes, some with superficial injuries and some with serious injuries, had begun to gather. Although Dr. Buck still had his black bag with him, he knew he needed medical supplies to treat the stream of injured being guided up the stairs to a makeshift clinic. He was also wise enough to know that the traumatized citizens needed a leader to tell them what to do next.

"Henry White," said Dr. Buck catching sight of his neighbor. "Go round up the boys and let's get to work." The American Legion Post officer did not have to question the order. He was out the door in a flash.

"Thomas," Buck continued, "you and the druggist go next door and salvage any type of medicine you can find. I especially need alcohol to disinfect all these open wounds."

Some of the first patients to be brought up the stairs were Ernestine, Thelma and baby Robert who had been discovered still tangled in the roots of the tree that had saved their lives. Thelma's foot had to be twisted out of the tentacles of the roots and she had a nail driven into her knee. Baby Robert's life was saved when the ersatz nurses in the hotel gave him periodic sips of whiskey and rubbed his body with whiskey swabs. He later nearly died from pneumonia.

"Doc, you should have seen it; it was just awful," babbled a man dragging what remained of the rest of his family into the clinic. "They was piled up there, you know, black and white together, and their eyes were open and...and...it was like you could still hear them screaming, Doc, but they was dead...lined up as far as we was able to see all along the banks and streets, Doc, and...dead, all of them." The man broke into heaving sobs as his wife placed her arm around his shoulders.

They were only the first such fractured families to come into the hotel with their injured, almost dead, lost and sobbing family remnants and telling a similar story. Many came in alone because they had no friends or family members left. Dr. Buck assured them all that help was on its way from West Palm Beach, and encouraged them to hang on. But there were no phones or radios, no intact roads or bridges, and the canals were clogged with wreckage. Nobody outside the Lake Okeechobee area knew what had happened in Belle Glade. No outside help of any kind was on its way.

It would be well into the following week before word of the devastation that had spread over the Lake Okeechobee region leaked to the outside world and roads and canals were cleared enough of debris that relatives and volunteers could move in and out of the area. The south Florida hurricane of April 16, 1928, is still known as the worst storm of the century because of the huge amount of property loss and the stunningly high number of lives lost when the water of Lake Okeechobee breached its earthen dike and flooded the entire area at the end of the lake.

That dreadful unholy Sabbath day in April of 1928 left the spirited pioneering people living near Lake Okeechobee brokenhearted for the rest of their lives and the Everglades changed forever.

HENRY MARTIN'S FAMILY: Henry Martin left the remainder of his family and friends resting in the hotel hospital and went out to search for his wife, Bessie Mae. Although he searched for days, he never saw his wife again. When he went to check out his farm, there was nothing left. It was as though his farm had never existed.

After time spent in a Miami hospital and then in a refugee house in Hollywood, he and his family finally returned to Belle Glade to begin all over again. He built another home, farmed his land and attempted to pull what was left of his family back together again. The storm had killed most of his spirit, however, and he lost his dreams of owning several stores and being the largest landowner in the Everglades. Henry never remarried.

HEARING THE LAND SPEAK

The proud, red stone walls of the canyon
speak to me, they know I hear their
murmur, their wisps of words
of ancient days where clouds came
to drain the sky, pulled rain in mists
against their blistered hot stones.

These slabs speak of one mighty
rushing river, heavy and deep rolling
in languid beauty, sparse grass,
tall willows bathed in dawn humidity.

The river nourishes white tailed deer;
bobcats on beaches roam where we can
track their path to water. Quietly I watch
a crow dip for his drink.

Listen, can you hear ancient shouts
ring out, echo, bombard with staccato
sounds, hit walls, bounce, echo again
just as darkness drops its heavy curtain
across canyons—is absolute until stars
break silvered light as cover for the night.

Marilyn Ball

REMEMBERING GRANDPA

Wendy Lambert

I N RESPONSE TO MY GREETING, his cloudy eyes look in my direction and he smiles as if he knows me. I push his wheelchair from the line of dozing patients sitting across from the nurse's station.

"He didn't eat his breakfast this morning," the nurse mutters as she studies his chart fastened to a clipboard. She turns her attention to an orderly and barks a series of orders, failing to offer the information which prompted my visit. He hasn't eaten anything since arriving at the nursing home two days ago.

I push him down the hall, looking for the small room he shares with another. The last room on the left. I wheel him in and sit on the bed opposite him.

"Are you hungry?" I ask.

He shakes his head no.

"This hotel has poor food and terrible service," he complains.

Rummaging through my bag, I pull out a peanut butter and jelly sandwich and place it into his shaking hands.

He feels the rounded corners of the sandwich; his eyes dimmed by age and disease. Immediately, he raises the sandwich to his lips and takes a bite. Grape jelly squishes from between the pieces of bread and clings around his mouth. He eats voraciously, barely swallowing before taking another bite. I hold a bottle of apple juice to his lips. Raising his fingers, he fumbles to secure the straw. His fingernails are long and ragged, yellow with age.

After he finishes a second sandwich, I place a small container of chips into his lap. With rhythmic strokes, he eats them one after another, only slowing when his fingers fail to clasp a chip.

I raise a napkin to his lips to wipe away the jam and crumbs and a trickle of drool nearing his chin. Satisfied he's eaten, I pluck a radio from the floor and press earbuds into his ears. I turn the dial knowing he'd love to hear some big band music, but I can't find any and settle on a classical music station instead.

He listens intently to the music, never breaching the silence except to cough. I grimace at the coughs. Though he smoked his last pipe more than twenty years before, the cancer had still come, ravaging both his lungs and mind.

Restless, he pulls the earbuds out and holds them for me to take. He tells me he's done listening. Grandpa's roommate is wheeled into the room and an orderly and a person, who appears to be the man's wife, move him into his bed with a great deal of effort. The man looks to be some thirty years younger than grandpa.

"Do you remember you taught me to fish at Hat Creek?" I ask.

Even though he doesn't look my direction, his face fans into a smile. He remembers Hat Creek. I remind him how we sat next to the river for hours, enjoying the peaceful rush of the creek and each other's company. I only pulled one fish from the creek that whole day.

I remind him of the afternoons he spent teaching me to oil paint on his deck beneath a canopy of evergreen trees filled with chattering squirrels. As his face continues to lighten, I press onward with memories of the raccoons that frequented his yard and the camping trips and long walks and card games and cups of hot chocolate and stories of the war.

His smile fades and face darkens.

"How do you know so much about my family? Who are you?" he asks.

My smile fades.

He asks about the doctor in New Jersey and if the test results are in.

I tell him I don't know about any doctor in New Jersey, but I know about the test results. I pause, reluctant to remind him of the truth—there is no cure for the cancer. He is going to die.

He nods. "I've lived a good, full life," he says tenderly. "It's okay."

My sister told me she'd found him clinging to his walker wandering the halls the night before. He tells me he was lost in Sunnyvale, searching desperately to find his new home.

"The houses all looked the same and I couldn't remember my phone number," he tells me earnestly. He'd wandered around the neighborhood for hours before a nice couple brought him home. I nod, unsure if I should humor this "memory" or not.

Shifting away from Sunnyvale, I talk about the trips to San Francisco and weaving down Lombard Street and walking along Fisherman's Wharf. He grins. We pass the next couple of hours, me feeding him memories of our summers together, him smiling. Silence lingers between the memories, punctuated by his coughs and the gurgle of his sleeping roommate.

I touch his hand and tell him it's time for me to go. With reluctance, I gather my bag and stare at my grandpa. He is now a shadow of his former self. A man caught up in a mix of memories both real and created. He is no longer the boy who'd survived the Great Depression by delivering milk in the middle of the night to aid his family. No longer the young soldier who'd fought bravely in the South Pacific in World War II. No longer the husband and father he'd once been. No longer the cantankerous grandpa who'd taught me so much.

"Is that you, Wendy?" he asks and turns towards the sound of my voice.

"Yes, Grandpa, it's me," I tell him. I smile and choke back tears.

He remembers.

RAIN

Wind whispers through blades of grass
Waves of heat mirage the field
Through the trees the moisture will pass
The air around congealed

Clouds melt out of the sky
Rain drops pull down the leaves
Making the flowers cry
Tears splash along the path it weaves

Seeping deeper the droplets flow
Between the muddy earth
Yearning for the sun to show
To ascend into the sky with mirth

Rising up the water will cling
Waiting to fall again and sing

Melanie Fowler

A BROTHER'S RESOLVE

Chris Todd Miller

"DAMN IT," DALE WHISPERED.

The canvas tent above him hung low with accumulated snow. He pushed himself onto one elbow and let his blanket fall. The cold morning air bit at the exposed skin of his neck and chest. He ran his hand along the canvas, cold and coarse on his fingers, feeling the weight of the snow. With a slight push, the snow slid off and landed with a soft *whump*. Frustrated, he looked over at his younger brother. Jacob had the blanket pulled up tight around his chin and his unruly curls splayed about the bedroll. He'd have Jacob stake the tent again, and this time he'd make sure it was done right.

Near the tent flap, his breath became visible. He pulled the canvas aside. A pristine blanket of snow covered the area. In the rising sun, he could barely make out the undulations of the battlefield in the valley below. If his fingernails weren't stained with blood and gunpowder, he might have convinced himself Old Man Winter was playing a trick on him and those mounds concealed by the snow weren't corpses.

More snow meant more mud. He actually didn't mind the cold as much as the mud. The mud turned everything ugly—it made everything the same; the cold kept him sharp. The languorous Kentucky sun would loll a man to sleep, make him slow and dumb. He didn't mind too much, though. Slow and dumb had brought about the demise of many a Confederate soldier.

It wouldn't be long before the sun chased the snow away and ushered in the mud. It was March and the weather in March was as unpredictable as Jefferson Davis's Rebels. Once the bodies thawed, the flies would come, and the maggots and beetles would render the flesh, and the bravado of young men, fodder for daylilies and marjoram.

To what end?

The sergeant broke Dale's trance. He'd forged a fresh trail of footprints to their tent. "The lieutenant wants to see you and Jacob."

Dale nodded.

Jacob rustled in his bed roll and mumbled something.

Dale didn't respond and Jacob spoke again. "Close the flap. It's as cold as a witch's tit out there."

Dale let the flap fall back into place. He never understood how Jacob could be more disturbed by physical discomforts than acts of battle. Faced with scenes straight out of Dante's *Inferno*, Jacob never complained or hesitated to act. For Dale, such images tormented his dreams.

Jacob longed for assignments most men feared and there was no shortage of fear. For this, he'd been singled out repeatedly by their superiors, receiving commendations and promotions. Most of the men looked up to him, even though he was several years their junior. The snow would be particularly upsetting to Jacob. Dale would enjoy telling him.

"Jacob," Dale barked.

"What?" he asked, his voice muffled by sleep and a dirty wool blanket.

"Get up. The lieutenant wants to see us." He paused. "And we've got snow."

"Ah, hell. I hate snow."

Dale smiled.

Jacob walked a step behind Dale as they trudged to the lieutenant's tent. Around them, the tents of their Union brothers rustled. The sounds of camp waking up—kindling snapping, pots clanking, and men cursing—punctuated the air.

"Aside from this cursed snow, what's on your mind this morning, brother? I can see your wheels turning," Jacob said.

After a moment, Dale responded. "It's just not like I thought it would be."

"Thought what would be?"

"All this, everything. For one, I thought this little skirmish with the South would be over long ago. When we enlisted, I saw us driving out the Rebels like a fox from a hen house and coming home heroes. I remember standing in the taverns and the assembly halls listening to all the rhetoric. I know better now. It doesn't matter how many we kill, those southern boys just keep comin'. This fight won't end until we're all dead."

"Here we go again," Jacob said. "Why you gotta talk like that?"

"Like what?"

"The war won't go on forever. You should take advantage of it while you can."

"Take advantage of what? An early grave?"

Jacob shook his head. "You never could see the fun in anything, not even when we were kids."

"You're not even eighteen," Dale said.

"And twenty-one makes you old and wise. Sorry, I forgot."

"You do realize were in the middle of a war, right? Not what most people would call fun."

They walked in silence for a moment.

"I'm not an idiot," Jacob said. "I see the lice and the blood and the bodies ripped apart, and that's not *fun*. But sometimes, when one of those Confederate boys dashes across a field or tries to collect surplus ammo—and we all take pot shots at him—that is kind of fun. Sure beats the hell out of plowing fields and shoveling manure."

Dale shook his head.

"Ah, yes, dour Dale. Ever the woe begotten. We're doing more living in a war than we ever did back home. All anyone every does back there is read and talk, mostly about the war. We live it. When we get back, we'll be in those taverns telling the stories that make men jealous and girls wet. Bonafide heroes is what we are."

Dale shook his head, again. They stopped in front of the lieutenant's tent. "Go on, hero, I'll wait for you here."

Jacob ducked into Lieutenant Sharp's tent, leaving Dale standing in the snow. The smell of cornmeal biscuits and coffee wafted past him and his stomach cussed him out for being negligent. Dale squinted into the sun and stamped his feet. He was about to abandon his post and fetch a cup of coffee and a johnnycake when Jacob emerged.

Dale looked at the smile on his brother's face. Uneasiness fell over him as a gust of icy wind whipped around him. "I've seen that look before. Nothing good comes from that look." He started toward the tent when the lieutenant's aid stepped out and stopped him. "Lieutenant says he'll get with you later."

Dale nodded and turned to Jacob, who could hardly contain himself. "All right, what?"

"Well," Jacob started, "see, there's this big battle that's gonna happen."

Dale waited wondering what his little brother had gotten himself into this time.

"So big that they're bringing together regiments from all over."

"You're not telling me anything I haven't heard before," Dale said.

"I know, I know. Hold your horses. This ain't no ordinary battle. Lieutenant Sharp says it could change the whole complexion of the war."

"Complexion. That was his word, right?" Dale asked.

"Will you just hush? He says, General Grant," Jacob paused for effect, "*General Grant* needs a special kind of soldier. Someone who can outrun and out-fox the Rebels."

"Why'd Lieutenant Sharp call you, then?" Dale turned and headed for coffee.

Jacob caught up to Dale in a couple of strides. "Haven't you noticed that the camp is packing up? We're pulling out to combine forces with General Grant at Petersburg and attack the Confederate capitol in Richmond."

"Damn it, Jake. Would you get to the point before I knock your head clean off?"

"All right, all right. Geesh, someone got up on the wrong side of the bed this morning. Here it is. I get to carry the Stars and Stripes into this monumental battle."

Dale stopped. "The blood cloth? The hell you are."

"The hell I am."

Dale felt his face flush. He could either walk away or knock some sense into his little brother. He chose to walk.

"This ain't like back home, Dale. You don't get to tell me what to do."

After three steps, he turned back to Jacob. "Boy, you're as stupid as you are brave. You know why it's called that, right? The blood cloth?"

Jacob scowled. "If you weren't my brother, I'd—"

"Do you ever pay attention? Or are you too busy having *fun* and collecting medals to see what's right in front of your face?"

"I know what this is. You're jealous," Jacob said. "Jealous that your little brother is a better soldier than you. And you know what else? I think that you're jealous that General Grant picked me."

"If that's what you think, then it's the stupidest thing to ever to escape your lips."

Jacob's face became hard, his eyes narrowed into slits. "It's an honor to raise the Stars and Stripes and nobody as young as me has ever done it before. Ask yourself this, big brother: why have they never asked you to do it?"

"Are you calling me a coward?"

A number of men stopped their preparations and gathered around Dale and Jacob.

Dale pointed to the valley of fallen soldiers hidden by the night's snowfall. "You see that? That field is full of brave men. There's a difference between brave and stupid. Guess which one's you."

Jacob yelled and drove his shoulder into Dale's gut, propelling the two of them to the ground.

The men started shouting, rooting for their favorite guy.

Dale got his hand under Jacob's chin and forced him back far enough to land a strike on Jacob's ribs. Jacob clutched his side and knocked Dale's arm from his chin. The two of them rolled in the snow and exchanged blows until the sergeant pushed through the crowd of men and pulled Dale off his brother.

"That's enough! You're both going on report, you dumb sons-o-bitches," the sergeant said.

Jacob pushed through the crowd and headed back toward their tent. Dale watched him go then turned back the way they'd just come.

Dale retraced the steps the sergeant had taken that morning. The sun reflected off the snow and into his eyes. Their tent was gone. Jacob stood next to their gear, packed and ready. Dale's knapsack sat on the ground waiting for him.

"Because of all the men who've died carrying it," Jacob said. "That's why the regiment flag is called a blood cloth. Those were brave men, Dale, the bravest. I would consider it an honor to add my name to theirs."

Dale let out a long sigh. "I don't think you really mean that. I think you believe it won't happen to you. You've done some amazing things, I'll admit. You should've died a number of times already, but you don't get it. Those Dixie boys would sooner take out the Stars and Stripes than General Grant himself. If you kill one man—even a leader—he's still just a man. When you take down a flag, you take down everything it represents. Hell, our guys do the same thing."

Jacob stood with his arms crossed. "I want to do this. I believe in everything our flag represents. You think I don't know it's dangerous? I'm not an idiot."

"Do you know what I believe in? I believe the rhetoric, Jacob. I believe in democracy, just like our kinfolk did in the face of King George. I believe that change comes from hard work, education, and sacrifice to build a truly civil society." He turned to the valley where so many of their Union brothers slept beneath the snow. "A society that would keep our kin from ending up like them."

He turned back to look Jacob in the eyes, and found them full of resolve. "I didn't even make a dent, did I?"

"I'm strong. I'm quick. I'm smarter than you think I am, and I've got one thing no flagman has ever had."

"Really? What's that?"

"I've got you, watching out for me."

Dale shouldered his pack. "You're right about that. I just had a long talk with the lieutenant."

"What did you say?" Jacob asked.

Dale could see the anger rising in his face. "I convinced him that you're more valuable among the ranks."

"You can't do that!" Jacob yelled.

"I already did, little brother. I promised Momma I'd bring you home safe and I will."

Jacob's face shook with anger. "I hate you."

When the company broke camp and headed east for Richmond, Dale still hadn't found Jacob. It felt odd to travel by himself. The muddy blue coats of the men marching on all sides penned him in, but Dale barely noticed—he kept looking for Jacob. Night after night, Dale slept alone in their tent right up until the morning of the attack.

The pre-dawn light cast an ironic serenity on the battlefield. Golden hues danced across the loaded muskets as the Union troops awaited Grant's battle charge. A dark line of Confederate troops stood in shadow, waiting for the sun to fully reveal them. Dale pressed the cold steel of his musket against his cheek. For the first time since they left Kentucky, Dale's eyes lighted upon Jacob.

He and Jacob always fought side by side, but this time Jacob stood about fifty yards ahead of him. In his head, Dale pleaded with Jacob to look back at him, just once.

One day little brother, your sons will thank me for what I've done.

General Grant signaled the command to advance. The troops responded, moving forward in a wave of blue. Everyone cried out as the battalion advanced on the Confederate troops. Various clusters of men broke off from the main swell to take on advancing foes. The zip of musket balls buzzed around him as Dale tried to advance and watch Jacob at the same time. He pushed past the soldiers around him, selfishly ducking behind them, using them for shields as he advanced.

"Jake!" Dale could barely hear his own voice over the din of musket fire and cannon.

He'd cut the distance between them in half.

He screamed his brother's name with such force it ripped at his throat. His cry swirled about him then fell to the cacophony of gunfire. Dale pushed past some soldiers from his regiment. Men he'd laughed with, shared stories of female conquest, and fought next to in his haste to catch up to Jacob.

I promised Momma.

The war cry of the man next to him stopped abruptly. Dale looked at the soldier and saw that most of his head was gone, leaving only remnants of the jaw and neck.

Jacob was close now, maybe only fifteen yards ahead, but he was only a few yards from the flagman. "Jake! Jake, hold up."

A tattered Stars and Stripes, hoisted by a new flagman, marked the give and take of the front line, until Old Glory fell. Jacob looked back and met Dale's eyes for an instant, then he darted forward.

Through the smoke and dirt, Dale saw the blood cloth rise again, right above Jacob's unruly curls. He lost sight of his brother when a cannon ball ripped open the ground, spraying dirt into his face. A man, caught in the blast, slammed into Dale, knocking him to the dirt. Wiping the grit and gore from his face, Dale recognized the man as Private Jefferies. Most of Private Jefferies's insides were now outside.

Jacob raised the Stars and Stripes and led the troops deeper into the fray.

"Jacob, wait!"

Musket balls continued to cut the air and more soldiers fell.

Jacob pressed forward and Dale felt pride well within him.

He lost sight of his little brother in the wave of the attack, but concentrated on the flag pitched above the troops. Abruptly, the flag disappeared. It resurfaced a moment later, but Dale fixed on where it had fallen.

Dale knelt beside his brother. He lay in one of the few grassy patches amid the dusty field.

Jacob tried to speak, but coughed up blood instead.

Dale gathered him in his arms. "Don't try to talk, Jake. Everything's gonna be all right. Just hang in there." Dale counted three wounds: one in the right shoulder, a second that had torn through his thigh, and the third embedded in his torso, likely piercing the lung. Dale picked him up under his arms to drag him out of the battle.

He stumbled and fell, gathered Jake again, and pulled him back behind the troops.

Jacob spit up more blood. His wounds had seeped to where they nearly filled the front of his uniform. The blood was warm and slick on Dale's hands.

"Stay with me, Jake."

"It's okay," Jacob said. "I did it. They's afraid, Dale. I could see it in 'em."

"Yeah, you're right, little brother, they're afraid."

A cannon ball pierced the air around them, then showered them with dirt.

"Tell Momma I'm sorry. That it weren't your fault." His chest bucked and the muscles in his face and neck seized.

Dale wanted to scream, no. That Jacob could do it himself.

It came out a whisper. "Stay, Jake, please."

He looked to the battle and saw that the blood cloth had enlisted a new soldier to lead the troops all while claiming another brother— his brother.

With two fingers he closed Jacob's eyes. "I'll tell Momma. I'll tell her how you chased off those yellow cowards. How they fled before you. I'll tell everyone about my brother—the hero."

DAY'S END

Sun going down, gold spangling the clouds,
my old chestnut standing on a grassy knoll,
head down, pulling grass.

We both enjoy this peaceful lull
at the end of a hard-sweating day.
And that's no understatement—
After bucking bales or hauling hay,
or eating dust kicked up
by ruddy steers and renegade cows,
(or flung up on my sunburned face
by tractors, horses, plows),
sometimes a man
needs to ponder...

I sit here on my pony
and gaze as far as I can see out yonder,
past the fields and high above mesas,
spellbound, 'cause even them poetic phrases
can't call to mind the peace
that's painted there by and by
when Nature's canvas
is a vast expanse of sky.

⌐*Sharon Nauta Steele*

CRY BOY THUNDER

Isaac Timm

AUGUST 8, 1985; 3:00 A.M.

THE RAIN COMES in intermittent waves, as does the smell of earth and dust purified. Sometimes a brief rattle of hail but mostly the roaring of devil blue fire, I turn up the radio but the station out of Oklahoma City, bounced into the western desert only at night, hisses and snaps. Little Richard's jubilance is muted, sinisterly buried under the static shadow of the thunderstorm. The trailer shakes and my thoughts are interrupted by roaring. There is no pause after the light as the beast stalks around the house, no time to count the seconds between the light and bellowing scream; the lightning and the thunder are the same. The attack is wave after wave of neon violet that comes through the window and down the dark hall to our bedroom. Next to me, my brothers are phantoms; their sleeping forms appear and disappear in the thunderstorm. They are asleep under its spell.

The music cuts out, the plain 1950's stenciled letters and numbers of the old radio die out in a slow green fade. The music of that age dies in a wink. The darkness lets out a breath then lights up like an arc welder and explodes. There is a smell of shattered stone or of fused earth. A stroke has exploded overhead, above the frail mantle of trailer roof. I lurch over the edge of the bed, trying to climb under; to make a cocoon under the mattress. I cry, I wail, lit by the rumbling strobe.

FEBRUARY 14, 1985; 10:00 A.M.

The light in the hall is glaring white florescent. My parents and I follow the yellow line down the hospital hall to the neurology department. I drank too much soda and need to find a bathroom. Our trip to the hospital started at 3:00 this morning, the University of Utah Hospital in Salt Lake City is six hours away from our small town of Callao.

It is the third time in four months we have traveled to a Salt Lake City hospital. The first visit was to Primary Children's, where a young woman doctor stripped me naked and felt my legs and measured my shoulders. She then let me put on pajamas and play on a big indoor swing, which was pretty cool. The second time, my first time at "The U," as Dad calls it, was not as fun. They glued little cardboard circles to my chest; each circle had a cold metal nipple that shivered the skin and the glue smelled horrible. They also drew vial after vial of cranberry blood from my arm then tried to placate me with a Flintstone's bandage. The call for the third visit was an unpleasant surprise for my parents. They were so annoyed at the expense of another trip that they shut the door to their bedroom when they took the call.

Three days later they are not much better. We spent six hours in the car listening to talk radio and grave silence. The gray February sky does not help their nerves. When we reach the hospital, they question the woman at the information desk in short sharp sentences. They ask where we need to go. The gray-haired informant tells us to follow the yellow line; it will lead us to neurology. I tell my parents we are like Dorothy and the Cowardly Lion; they do not laugh. When we get there, they talk to the doctor about tests. I lean back yawning. I'm really bored. I start panning my head from side to side to count the ceiling tiles while opening and closing mouth to make wet "gop" noises.

"Oh, for heck sake, Zeke," my mother hisses, "go find a bathroom already."

After I am finished, I turn the corner into the hall. Fifteen feet ahead, my parents and the doctor speak in hushed tones. My mother is pleading, red faced, stripped of edifice; the doctor returns her words in clipped professional jargon and turns, walks down the hall and enters the next office where another family waits. My mother crumples, all the pins knocked from her scaffolding, and she cries. I am torn, I want to run to my mother to comfort her, but I also want to leap into my father's arms. I rush forward, but only five steps. I see my father and stop but my dad is not there. There is another man with the same eyes, face, height and build of the father. But that father does not cry; he is mountain strong. This man's eyes are stricken and his hands are quivering white fists. Is he mad at me? Then his eyes land on mine and he waivers, almost falling. Something crumbles into my heart and belly, quick lime that creates a stone. It would be better if he were angry.

MAY 15, 1985

We are gathering money for Jerry's Kids. It is a new club that I am part of. If I collect enough donations, I win the king of all prizes, a Sony Walkman. The shiny black machine that hides behind electronic store Plexiglas, to be marveled at briefly before our parents hauled us to the thrift store to try on stiff, uncomfortable jeans.

My parents and I get into the Ford Ranger with the gray fender and bounce down Callao's main road, which is really just tan, packed dirt that breeds ruts. The first house, after my Aunt Barbara's, is the Garland's house. They have a porch that I love because it smells of grapes, but we can't talk on the porch. In Callao money talk is for living rooms.

The living room is made dark blue as the sunlight bleeds the color of the heavy lace curtains onto the walls and floor. An old maple piano gives the room the guise of a museum; on top of it are brass oil lamps whose polished surfaces reflect the various figurines that share their perch. Mrs. Garland lets me sit in the old rocking chair that reminds me of a sled with long walnut runners. It has large macramé cushions wove with tiny red roses and impregnated with the scent of lilacs. I sit politely as I can, barely containing the urge to rock back and forth as fast as I can.

My parents show them the brochure. There is a picture of some old guy named Jerry Lewis who likes to make constipated faces; he is some kind of actor. There is also a boy with him in a wheelchair. The picture is wrong. The boy is too skinny, his jaw doesn't sit right and his arms are like sticks. There is some kind of hose that goes into a white collar around his neck, but I know that under that collar the hose is penetrating his skin; the rumble returns to my stomach. My parents converse with the Garland's in quiet tones. Every once in a while Mr. Garland looks at me solemnly and contemplates.

He is a leather man, a tough man; he looks at me around a bushy, low-hanging cowboy mustache. In his eyes is quiet sorrow. After a while he writes out a check to my father and signs the donations slip. He offers me a soda. I say no thanks. (I have a rumble stomach.) A cold, sneaky whisper enters my brain, telling me we aren't collecting money to give to Jerry's Kids. It's not for Jerry Lewis at all. The money is for the boy who has a hose in his throat, that disjointed puppet, the boy who I will become. My mouth is dry as alkali; in my head is the buzzing of wasps. I wish I'd taken the soda.

JULY 21, 1985

I tear the box out of my mother's hands; the cardboard is still warm from the summer sun. With a savage will I shred the outer shell, sending pieces of box and foam peanuts into the air in a destructive fountain. Inside the cardboard ruin is a second box. Turning it over in my hands, I enjoy the squeaking newness of the thing. I slowly open the inner box as if it were a sacred relic, not wanting to tear even one of its shimmering tabs. The Walkman slides out in a Styrofoam tray and it smells of electric glory. I rip open the plastic that wraps it with my teeth and pour the warm black jewel into my hands. I set it on the floor and then strip out the Walkman's other parts and set them around it. I stare at the whole glorious prize. My mind slips the clutch as a realization comes to me: this is not just a prize, it's the best prize; the number one. The full heavy matter takes me between the eyes. My neighbors, family and friends, are the reason I have this object; but not for this object. Their hard-earned money, cash from breadboxes, shoeboxes; checks signed with hands covered in axle grease. The Walkman is suddenly a smaller thing, a cheap plastic token compared to the outpouring of neighbors' hope, that I would get well, that the boy on the brochures would be cured.

Wyatt spins on the porch; I hear four-clawed feet circling on the plywood floor. I'm still scared but I jump out of bed in my pajamas, stumbling at speed toward the door. I need to save my dog; he must be terrified. I open the door, prepared for the rush of small golden-white dog but the door is empty. I go to turn on the light but then remember that the power is out. I look around in the almost complete darkness for a flashlight. There is a flash of blue and I see my dog briefly standing on his back legs with is front paws leaning on the door. He is looking at me with the stub of his tail wagging. It goes dark again and he barks demandingly from the void.

"You want to go out?" I blurt with a loud squeak.

Out into the yard the scents of wet earth and orchard grass assault me. After the darkness of the house the outdoors is illuminated. The boiling thunderheads and shadow mountains cross-hatch into shades of gray only to suddenly explode into a blue world. The bolt fans out across the horizon in fourteen different points; this is followed by others in a five-second light show. My hold to the door-frame iron, my knees jelly. Wyatt dances on the flagstone landing and whimpers like a child wanting to run. His alien joy is infectious. My hands disentangle from the door frame and my legs drag me down the wet cedar steps. The gray-flecked stones of the path feel warm under my bare feet. A brief flurry of fat rain drops pelts me but the drops are warm as if charged. Wyatt barks with glee and bolts out across the orchard. My legs are disconnected from my brain and I run at full speed after his low white form.

I burst through the current hedge that marks the boundary between orchard and garden; I trip on my way out of the leafy threshold only to fall prone into dark humps of dirt that smell of earth borne limes. I pull myself free to chase Wyatt through the summer squash but a bolt flashes and I throw myself to the ground for cover; as if there is protection in molten yellow gourds. The thunder rolls over. My heart pounds and my will nearly gives out. Then there is a gold muzzle in my face and Wyatt licks me with a large flat tongue. I sputter and curse, try to swat at him but he darts away nimbly. I get up to chase him, but he's already crossed the low gate that heads out into the expanse of field, to bark and do another spin.

"Come and get me, two legs," he mocks.

I rush out of the gate, leap the ditch and land barefoot in the alfalfa; I slip in the wet green plants. Wyatt's trail cuts a clear path through the wet shoots. I don't want to lose the trail so I don't brother to stand up. Just rush through the leafy green on all fours until the knees of my pajamas are soaked through with mud and my night shirt becomes nothing more than a wet rag. Wyatt begins to range further ahead me; I can hear his warthog snorts retreating. His four legs can just carry him further and faster.

I stand up to get my bearing and find myself deeper into the field than I thought. Our house and orchard shifts as a black outline in the wind. I see Wyatt at the western edge of the field, near an irrigation ditch with his nose to the ground, stopping once in a while to dig down with badger claws. Sticking his muzzle in the upturned earth and snorting a cloud of semi-wet dust. Our chase game has been replaced by the business of hunting gophers.

The thunder rumbles in the distance but I ignore it. To my right is a copper spun hay bale, abandoned from spring harvest. I take off my wet night shirt. The intermitting rain drops form a fine mist, a ground fog. The sky lights up again in an azure cascade. I throw myself jarringly into the alfalfa. Blue, black, blue, black; then waves of earth-shaking rumbles. When the roar fades I cautiously rise but trip on my pajamas and fall down. I curse and pull them off. I'm naked but don't care. Damn thunder, damn lightning; damn noise that sends me simpering to the earth. Seconds later, more lightning arcs across the sky but I am angry and do not budge. It spreads, covering the whole sky, trying to corral me with florescent fingers, to cow me with its rumbling. I roar back, my small yell but a piccolo to the bass drum. I jump up on the hay bale; the sharp straw ends bite my bare feet. I yell at the sky like an animal. Wyatt stops digging to stare up at me with unblinking eyes. The lightning lances in waves casting the mountains in neon relief but I scream unafraid. In my head I turn the thunder into a whisper. My voice is greater. I howl at the rain and the lightning; at the thunder, my pounding heart, my fear and sorrow. My boy lungs expand to take in the whole world and I shout in an unrecognizable bellow. Down with cold-eyed doctors! Down with cold gray Februarys and parents treating me with kid gloves. I am still Isaac; no machine will be attached to me. No more adult sorrow, no more jumping up when I fall, like I am made of glass. I roar, I shout, I am boy thunder; my anger lights up the west and my rage shakes the earth...

The air flames red and a there is a shockwave followed by an instant report that makes my ears ring. I am thrown from the bale. I get up slowly and then stare in shock. Ten feet from where I stand is a smoking circle that smells of earth and ozone. I do not think. I just grab my wet clothes and run full speed toward the house; in my mind are headlines: *Stupid Boy Struck by Lightning* or *Naked Corpse Found on Hay Bale; News at 11.* I fly through the fence and over the garden, crash through the current bushes without pause. My feet barely touch paving stone or steps as I leap up them into the house; they echo only twice on the wood floor of the porch. I throw the door open and shut it in one movement then fall to the dry carpet; feel its fibers on my naked back. My heart beats fast but I am not scared. I feel safe. On the porch I hear Wyatt curling up in his bed, through the house is the sleeping breath of brothers and parents.

AUGUST 8, 2003, NEVADA MORNING

My wife and I sit in our car; pulled off the road 25 miles west of Caliente, Nevada, on Route 95. In the southern part of the Great Basin the great thunderheads only drop their water half way. The rain evaporates before it hits the ground due to waves of desert heat. Every once in a while cold rain penetrates the air shield with fat drops, avenging itself with microburst fury. Only in the desert does rain kick up a dust.

Aaron lies back against me, her eyes track the lightning. She is silently counting, and I feel her shiver against me when the thunder peels.

"That was close," she whispers, as if thunderstorms are solemn communions. I peer out through the rain-streaked glass, hold her close, and take in the scent of her clean hair. I hold her close until the brief thunderstorm passes, then get out and stretch my road-weary legs. Compared to last year I'm a little worse for wear, can't drive as far as I'd wish without stopping to rest, but 1985 is long gone as are many projected death dates, 16, 21, and 30. The doctors have long since clarified my diagnoses as Becker's Muscular Dystrophy. I don't know if my physical therapist would have approved of this road trip, but Aaron makes sure I mind my "smaller battery" and keeps me from doing something bone-headed like taking stairs.

I reflect on the boy with the collar and its hose. I am not that puppet and either was he. He was my friend Jeremy, and he lived his short life well. Some that are healthy would say that I was lucky, to not have the type of muscular dystrophy that killed Jeremy, but they really don't have a damn clue. How lucky is it to bury a friend? I look at my wife, smile as I watch her enraptured face waiting for the next show, it is in this moment and moments like it that carries with it an understanding, one that Jeremy knew at only sixteen; that we are not unlucky but fortunate. That we are the few that know one free breath is worth a lifetime of worry. Will I run free as I did when I was ten and scream unashamed and defiant? No, but I will carry that spark for as long as I can. I am boy thunder and I am content. I get back into the car and whisper something in Aaron's ear, making her to smile. The storm starts up again and we watch the world explode in roaring brilliance.

DEPARTURE

Gingerly he crosses
on the uneven gravel,
afraid of falling
holding firmly to his cane.
Three months and three days have passed
since she departed,
leaving him behind, alone.
Sixty years ago,
they were so young, and in love,
pledged their vows so solemnly.

Oh, to return now
for one day or just an hour,
hold her in his arms,
tenderly express his love,
feel again her sweet touch.

Time is too cruel,
taking her away so suddenly
his dear companion.
He leaves a single daisy,
her favorite on the grave.

Lin Vernon Floyd

BIRTH

Emily Younker

THE WHEELS OF KIRA'S SKATEBOARD clacked in the cracks of the sidewalk as she rode to the university. Every so often she'd push off with her foot, just to get that extra burst of speed. She liked feeling the wind in her face since she practically cloistered herself during the school year. Traveling between home, school, and work was the only time she had to enjoy the air. The cool air brushing her cheeks this morning almost made forget the disastrous weekend.

She did it on a dare, a bit stupid for a twenty-one-year-old to accept the dare in the first place, but she did. Pay a buck. Prick your finger. Learn your cause of death. Simple. Almost painless. For Kira, however, it was more than that. It wasn't just learning her death. It was a realization that her life would only be looking around the corner for her death. That was why the paper with her fate remained stuffed in the back of her sock drawer.

"Kira, wait up."

Kira leaned back, bringing the board to a stop. She popped the deck and caught the end as it came up. Lance jogged up to her. They'd known each other in high school, and somehow their friendship had persevered through two years of college despite their differences in majors. Kira pursued a degree in finance while Lance reveled in the psychology department. After Friday night she wasn't sure he would come talk to her. Her heart fluttered for a moment, glad everything was back to normal.

"I can't believe you still ride that thing around," Lance said, adjusting his shirt after the quick jog.

Kira held the skateboard close for a moment, a look of mock shock on her face. She bumped her shoulder against his and continued walking towards campus. "I can't afford a car."

"Maybe if you didn't waste your money."

She didn't reply. Today she felt rich and probably could afford a junker of a car, but today was bill day. The Doppelt Company would call at five-thirty, so until then, she could pretend to be rich. Lance knew that she helped pay the monthly bills that plagued her parents.

The Doppelt Company provided medical technology. It was the only company that agreed to help her parents during her birth. They hadn't come cheap but they had helped when no one else would. Five years ago, when she went looking for them, their website had consisted of a phone number and their logo. Now they called on a monthly basis for her money, and it meant her parents didn't have to pay as much. They gave up more for her than she would ever be able to repay.

"Why not just walk?" Lance asked.

She laughed and turned to walk backwards in front of him. "Why walk when you can ride? I like the wind."

"It's going to be the death of you," Lance grumbled.

Kira winced. She didn't mean to. Her heel caught an uneven crack and she stumbled backwards. Lance's hand darted out and he grabbed her shoulder.

"Sorry," he said. "Poor choice of words."

"Don't worry about it," she said it with a smile, trying to bring back the light mood. But Lance wouldn't look at her.

It had been because of Lance she'd used the old machine in the arcade last Friday. It squatted in the corner of the room, lurking among the lights and sounds. Everyone who walked into the arcade stared at it for a moment, as if sizing it up, and then ignored it. Kira, Lance, and various other friends had been to the arcade dozens of times throughout high school. They too would stare at the machine and every time someone would say, "Fifty bucks." The others in the group would laugh and then everyone ignored it. As far as she knew, no one ever tried it.

Friday night it was just Lance and Kira. Technically, it was a date, but they both refused to call it that, just in case it went wrong. No need to panic.

"Fifty bucks," Lance said.

"Make it a hundred," Kira replied.

"Two-hundred," Lance said.

Kira raised an eyebrow and they both laughed. They moved further into the arcade making a beeline for the air hockey table.

"A thousand," said another voice.

Kira laughed and kept walking. Lance stopped.

"A thousand dollars?" he asked.

"For using the machine. Learning how you die," the man replied.

"Come on, Lance," Kira said, turning around to pull him with her.

She recognized the speaker as the arcade owner. He held up a wad of bills. The arcade was a whirr of colored lights and 8-bit sounds from the machines, but the people in the room remained still and silent. The man tossed the money to Lance. It was a fairly large stack and Lance flipped through it, looking at the different denominations of bills.

"It's yours, if you have the balls to prick your finger."

"Why?" she asked.

"Few people have ever touched the machine, but once someone does, everyone will."

Kira could see the gears in Lance's mind spinning. A thousand dollars for either of them would mean rent and food for at least two months. Or paying off more of the eternal medical bills from her birth. Lance didn't work. His school schedule was wonky, giving him an hour here or there, but not enough free time together for a job. The fact that he even considered the money made Kira shiver. He was broke and desperate.

"Fine," she said. "It's not like it's actually real."

A crowd condensed around her. She'd never seen the machine up close. The black and gold box stood to her shoulder. Dust clung to the surface, obscuring the writing on the top. Kira lifted her hand and brushed the dust away, hoping no one saw her hand shake.

1. Insert $1 into slot.
2. Press finger against pad.
3. Take fortune.
4. Enjoy the rest of your life.

"All I have to do is prick my finger?" she said.

The man let out a little smirk and nodded. She moved over to Lance who still clutched the stack of money.

"This is on you," she said and pulled out a worn dollar. Lance looked like he was going to protest. He reached for the money but then pulled it back. He ran his fingers along the edge of the stack.

The machine ate the dollar on the first try and a small, yellow square lit up on the front of the machine. Kira bit her lip but firmly pressed her left index finger against the square. The prick was quick but stung more than she anticipated. She pulled her finger away and stared at the small red dot in her flesh.

The black machine made no noise and nothing changed. After a minute of nothing, the machine beeped once. Nothing else happened. A small part of her wanted to cheer in relief as she turned towards the crowd.

"Done. Thanks for the money."

"Look," Lance said, his voice low. Resting in a small alcove was a square piece of white paper. It was blank. This time she was sure everyone could see her hands tremble as she picked it up. Her fingers felt the ridges of ink on the other side but she folded it quickly and stuffed it in her pocket.

"My death, my business," she announced. "Come on, Lance. Let's get out of here."

Lance trailed after her as she walked from the arcade on shaking legs. The arcade owner laughed, not seeming to care that he'd just lost a grand. But then again, people now flocked to the machine in droves. The now-officially-not-a-date-night ended five minutes later.

As Kira continued walking toward campus, she pushed the memory away. She tried to think of another conversation topic.

"Thanks for the money," Lance said for the hundredth time. "You sure you don't want it?"

She wanted it, but she didn't want it. If she took the money, she would always remember the square of paper. If Lance had it, she could forget it in time, hopefully. "I told you, keep it."

Lance fell silent and matched his stride to hers. Finally, he said, "Are you doing anything this weekend?"

"Not that I know of."

This time Lance winced. He looked ridiculous, and it made her sick that such a harmless comment would make anyone flinch.

Kira shook her head and stopped walking. Neither of them would forget and that would always be a barrier between them. "I can't handle this right now. Bye, Lance."

She dropped the skateboard to the sidewalk and pushed off. It wasn't as if the relationship would have gone anywhere, anyway. Kira knew she couldn't offer him everything needed in the way of girl-friend or later as a wife. Besides, paying for bills that sucked more than half of her income, an accident and subsequent surgery as a child left her physically incapable of getting pregnant. But, being barren wasn't as big as the money. Money would always be an issue. Having it or not having it. She kept telling herself that if Lance didn't care about the money, he wouldn't have accepted the thousand from her in the first place. He never even let her handle it.

In the first class of the day, her favorite class, she focused on the lecture through sheer willpower. In her general genetics class, she found herself doodling geometric shapes on the margins of the handouts.

"Earth to Kira. Come in, Kira."

Her elbow slipped and she looked up in surprise. Her professor stood in front of her, arms folded and tapping his foot.

"I see that you have decided to join us, finally."

"Sorry," she said and sat up straighter in the chair.

"Did you at least complete the reading assignment?"

Kira looked at her book and wracked her brain. She had read it, before everything happened over the weekend.

"Clones," she said after a painful silence. "It was talking about how to use DNA to create clones, like Dolly the sheep."

"Anything else that you can remember?"

"Human cloning is frowned upon?" She said.

"Something that isn't common knowledge?"

Kira shook her head, her face burning.

The professor frowned and moved back to stand in front of the class. "The term is derived from the Greek word for trunk or branch. There are several different types of cloning. Can anyone tell me what they are?"

A student in the back answered, "Molecular, cell, and organism."

Kira sagged back into her chair. She tried to pay attention for the rest of the class and by the time the lecture ended she was glad to be out of there. The ride to work, with the wind blowing in her face, wasn't nearly as calming as she hoped it would be.

At five o'clock, after her six-hour shift from Hades at the call center, Kira wanted to barricade herself in her apartment and never leave. Her first reaction to the awful day was to call Lance, but that option wasn't open anymore. She hated to mope and decided to do something about it. With a mug of hot chocolate, she curled up on the couch and called her father. Her parents had moved the year before to a smaller, cheaper apartment.

"Hello, Dad."

"What's wrong?"

With just the two words he had known something was wrong. She wondered if that was why she'd called him, because she wanted him to know.

"Nothing."

He chuckled and she could hear him sniff.

"I can smell the hot chocolate from here."

It made her laugh, and a small bit of tension eased from her shoulders.

"Is it Lance?" he asked.

"You can figure everything out without me saying anything."

"Not everything," he said. She could picture him smiling, his blue eyes squinting almost closed as he did. "Why don't you tell me?"

She swirled the dregs of the chocolate in her cup. The last few sips were always the richest.

"I broke up with Lance."

"Why?"

"I just can't do it. I can't give him what he wants."

"Just because you can't get pregnant doesn't mean you can't have children. You should know better than anyone."

Adoption was always an option and she had no qualms about it. She loved her two younger brothers though they shared no blood. She winced, wanting to tell him about the bills she helped pay, but she couldn't bring herself to. Now she sounded shallow. Kira was the oldest of three and the only biological child. During her delivery, complications arose. She and her mother almost died in the process. It was almost a year before Kira came home from the hospital. She'd been small for her age, but eventually caught up with everyone. Every three months she was supposed to have a checkup and the results were sent on to the Doppelt Company.

"There's something else that's bothering you."

She took a sip of the coco and the extra rich liquid settled in her stomach like molten lead.

"Have you ever heard of something called the Machine of Death?"

"Machine of Death?"

She waited, hoping he would say more, yet wanting to take back the words.

"Why do you ask?" he finally said.

"There's one in the arcade, remember?"

There was another pause before her father laughed. "That Machine of Death? It's nothing but a prank. It's like an emo version of the old fortune teller machines they use to make."

He laughed again and she wanted to laugh with him, but it stuck in her throat. The weight in her stomach only grew with everything he said.

"We used to tease each other to go try it. It doesn't even work."

"Doesn't work?"

"We couldn't even get it to take the money," her father's voice was light hearted, too light hearted and almost pleading. It didn't add up.

"I should go," she said. "Talk to you later." She hung up.

He wouldn't call back. Not right now, anyway.

She shuffled to her bedroom and lay on the bed, staring at the sock drawer. She couldn't decide what was worse, her father lying to her, or the fact that she knew the method of her death was written on a small piece of paper hidden in the back of her sock drawer. She tossed her phone on the pillow.

"How bad could it be?" she muttered and stood up, hand reaching for the drawer. "There's nothing to lose."

The phone rang. She didn't even look at it. Her courage faltered. The caller didn't leave a message. The phone rang again. She felt her determination slip with each ring. The caller never left a message. The fourth time the phone rang, she walked over and picked it up without looking at the caller ID. It was about time for the billing company to call.

"Hello?"

"Hi, honey. Am I interrupting something?"

"Mom?" Kira sat down on the bed and took a second to flip through her call list. Something was definitely wrong if her mother had called four times.

"I'm sorry to hear about Lance."

Kira flopped back on her bed.

"Maybe you should stay with us for a few days."

"I have school," Kira replied. "I can't commute three hours to school each day. I don't have a car."

"I don't—I guess you're right. Why don't we come up and visit you?"

Kira frowned as she looked around her small apartment. One bedroom, a bathroom, a small kitchen, and an equally small living room. Her parents couldn't afford a hotel, and there wasn't any room for them here.

"I'm fine. I'll come visit this weekend." She mentally added, "If I can find a ride."

"Are you sure you don't want us up there?"

"I'm fine."

The silence stretched over the phone and for a brief second she thought she heard her father in the background saying, "—couldn't know."

"See you this weekend," Kira said.

"Yes, of course. Make it a good week."

As soon as the call disconnected, Kira was on her feet. She pulled open the drawer and snatched the fortune. The folded paper was smooth against her fingers. She opened it, keeping the message turned away from her and once again felt the raised ink. It drew her and though she knew it would burn her, as a moth to the flame, she turned the paper over.

Birth.

Her fingers traced the five letters, the weight in her stomach turning and wrenching. The word tasted vile in her mouth. It was like a sick joke, someone who was unable to have children dying due to a birth, just like her mother almost did. A birth would cause her death. If the Machine of Death was real, anyway. Obviously she survived her own birth, and she was certain it was anatomically impossible for her to get pregnant and give birth. That didn't leave many other options.

Birth.

The phone rang again. She glanced at the caller id this time, Doppelt Labs, and flipped it open. This call she'd been expecting. They always called the first Monday of the month at five-thirty. Like clockwork. The only thing certain in life was death, taxes, and medical bill collectors. She swallowed at the thought of death and pushed the thought from her mind.

"Hello."

"May I speak to Kira Patterson?"

"This is her," Kira said. She knew the routine after doing this since she had her first job at sixteen.

"Has your account information changed?" the woman asked.

"No."

"How much would you like to pay this month?"

"Five hundred."

"Would you like us to mail the receipt to you, or would you prefer to get setup online?"

"Online?"

The woman's voice could be described as chipper as she spoke. "It is a new process we are implementing, to better serve our clients.

All of the bills can be managed through the secure server as well as tracking the progress of the work. If you have any complaints or questions, there is always someone monitoring the site that can be of help."

"I don't think I have the rights for that, you might as well just mail the receipt."

"Of course you have rights."

Kira frowned. "No, I don't. I'm an anonymous donor." She added half to herself, "But I turned twenty-one last month. Could that be it?"

"You are listed on the account. I'll get you setup so you can see."

Kira moved over to her computer and followed the directions. The website looked almost the same, the name and a phone number, but now there was a sign in and password box at the top of the screen.

"Please let us know if you have any questions. We are especially interested in hearing from you."

"Yeah," Kira said, already typing in the information. A new window opened.

She barely heard the woman say, "Have a nice day," and hang up.

"The Doppelt company: Leading the World in Organism Cloning," she said reading the new information on the website. She clicked on the billing tab.

She knew the bill had to be large. Her parents had been making payments for twenty years.

"A million dollars? They paid a million dollars? For what?"

She clicked through the payment tabs looking at the number decrease from her own petty contributions and her parents' payments. They still had a long way to go. Maybe she could set aside eight-hundred each month.

Another link caught her eye.

"Notes," she read.

It looked like a blog, lines of text separated by dates. The date on top was from two months earlier. Her last doctor's appointment.

"Subject coping with extended stress of adult life. Vitals are in the normal expectancy range."

The next dozen entries were similar. She scanned down to a bigger paragraph of text.

"Subject entered the workforce. Worried about stress that comes from training. After three weeks patient shows exhaustion but body is coping well. All within range."

Further down she read.

"Setback in research. Subject suffered from internal injuries after being hit by a car. Surgeon removed reproductive organs that were damaged beyond repair. Will not be able to test theory of normal reproduction in Subject."

Birth.

Kira covered her mouth with a shaking hand. She scrolled down to the last entry on the page. Her birth date.

"Family made inquiry after daughter died due to complications from birth. DNA sequence retrieved from Kira Zero. Cloning process of Kira Prime to begin immediately."

SNOW

Snow
Soft, silent
Falling, fleeting, melting
Gentle dancing quiet flakes
Winter

⤴Ruth Asay

THE SUNDAY FUNNIES

Amanda Luzzader

I PEER OUT THE WINDOW AGAIN, but nothing changes. Today, no news is bad news.

To call our paperboy mediocre would be kind. I've plucked our newspaper out of bushes and trees. Dragged it out from under cars. On rainy days, soggy bundles have gone straight from porch to trash bin. Even when it's sunny, if there's a puddle, that kid will find it.

Sometimes the front page will be shredded after the paper is strangled with not one, but five elastic bands. Other days, the pages are left free to blow in the wind. I'm often torn between wanting to be an informed citizen and not wanting to be the crazy neighbor chasing paper through the streets.

For the longest time, I actually thought our paper was being swiped. I gave the neighbors the stink-eye every chance I got. It wasn't until I phoned the paperboy to see if he'd seen anything suspicious that I discovered there'd been no paper to steal. He'd just been "tired" and "busy."

Worried it's one of those days, I go outside and walk around like I'm conducting my own personal Easter egg hunt. But other than a broken Frisbee, there's nothing newsworthy. We've already made a couple complaints over the last few months that have yielded little improvement. This time, I'm determined to speak with the distribution manager.

I want the paper to know just how bothered I am. So first, I call for reinforcement.

Mom's a fiery redhead who has spent decades working in the legal field. She's an expert on litigation. One time I tried to use a coupon when we were out shopping together. The store employee told me there'd been a printing error and the discount wasn't valid. Mom's eyes darkened and she went into a rant about false advertising and lawsuits and the store losing way more than the measly amount on the coupon. By the time she was finished I'm sure the employee would've given it to us for free, just to be rid of us. I got my discount. Mom's a bulldog when it comes to her pups. If there's anyone who can sound the battle cry, it's Mom.

"I know he's only thirteen, but they shouldn't hire someone so young if he can't do the job."

"You're right," Mom says quietly.

I walk around the room, gesturing with my hands. "It's not like this is the first time either. And today it's the Sunday paper—I'm missing all the extra ads and wedding announcements and the Sunday funnies."

"Mm-hmm."

I frown. "You sure you're okay?"

"It's your dad," she tells me. "He's gone to Insta-Care with some chest pains."

"Probably indigestion." I shrug.

"Maybe. I just can't think of what we ate."

Everyone in my family suffers from a mild form of hypochondria. All I have to do is see a news report on an illness to start feeling feverish. We visit the doctor too much. I'm not concerned, but I tell Mom to let me know what the doctor says anyway.

I hang up the phone and walk away. After Mom's underwhelming response, I decide to give the kid one more chance.

A few hours later, Mom calls back. They've sent Dad to the emergency room to do some blood tests; she's meeting him there. She says not to worry. I don't.

Fifteen more minutes. The phone rings again. Dad's having a heart attack.

I sink into our couch. "Should I come?"

"No—you've got Hudson."

Hudson, my eighteen-month-old son is quite mobile, but not verbal. He doesn't respond to the word "no." My husband's not home, so if I go, I'd have to bring Hudson. I can picture him running through the halls of the hospital, tipping over trays, dumping drawers, and hiding in other patients' rooms.

"You sure?"

"Yeah, just enjoy your evening."

I hang up and stare at the phone in my hands. *Enjoy my evening?* Things must really be bad.

Before I can make any decision, the phone rings again. This time there's no greeting, just an intake of air. My chest tightens.

"Mom?"

"They're life-flighting him to McKay-Dee."

"I'm coming."

⤸

At the emergency room, a nurse points me down the hall, but I can already see Dad through his door.

Reclined in a hospital bed, he raises his hand off the blanket in a weak wave and smiles sheepishly. It's only been a week since I've seen him, but he seems smaller.

You shouldn't have come, a voice in my head says. *If you hadn't come, he'd be tall and strong forever.*

Inside the room are three chairs, but no one's sitting in them. A neighbor of my parents is leaning against the wall. Mom's pacing the floor. Her eyes are red-rimmed, but her face is dry. A smile, like the ones found at car dealerships and beauty pageants, is fixed on her face.

"Wasn't it nice of Albert to come?" she asks. Her smile grows to jack-o'-lantern proportions, making me wonder about my own expression.

My face has become a device. In my novice hands, I could easily make a mistake. If I smile to show support, will Dad think I don't care? If I look too upset, will that distress him? I stare at the ground and try to clear myself of any emotion until I can decide how to present myself. The floor has white tiles with gray speckles. My lips and eyebrows move to neutral territories.

Hudson wriggles in my arms. I'd thought about leaving him with someone, but I'm glad I didn't. We all are.

He's the only one in the room who's transparent. He isn't thinking or remembering or masking. He's just being. He's too small to see the elephant.

Freed from my arms, he scrambles to the base of my father's hospital bed.

"Sure getting big," the neighbor says.

I nod.

"Hudson, look at Papa's bed," my mom says. "See those buttons? His bed can go up and down!"

Mom lifts Hudson and settles him in next to Dad.

"They've been picking on me, Hudson." Dad exaggerates a frown. "See this I.V.? They've been poking Papa."

"I'm glad you brought him," Mom whispers to me as Dad tussles Hudson's hair. "That's the best your dad's looked all day."

His best doesn't look good. Rosy cheeks have turned pallid, with chapped lips fading into his pale skin. In the oversized hospital gown, he looks weak and vulnerable. Dad was always the one I'd call when I needed heavy lifting but now he's barely holding himself up.

Soon, my sisters arrive and then my husband. The small room is filled. It's like some weird party—our whole family there, chitchatting, smiling.

Nurses come. They check readings and monitors. Take his blood pressure. While they work, I study Dad. A perfectly round face, dimples, and the bluest eyes I've ever seen—a pool with no end. I know I'm staring, but it feels like I haven't really looked at him in years.

Word finally comes; the helicopter's here. Everyone except Mom steps into the hall so Dad can have some privacy as they move him to a gurney. A curtain is pulled across the doorway.

My husband, Ross, puts Hudson on his shoulders. The last time any of us were at the hospital was when Hudson was born, my parents' first grandchild. I always thought we were lucky to live so close to my parents—for my kids to be able to have a relationship with them. We eat Sunday dinner together at their house every week.

After a few minutes, the curtain opens. We squish against the wall as the helicopter crew maneuvers the stretcher into the hall. They clear the doorframe and begin to jog. My heart accelerates. I'd waited in that little room with my dad for forty-five minutes, but now they're running. Maybe I'm naïve or maybe just inexperienced, but I'd honestly thought we'd all walk to the heli-pad together, taking turns holding Dad's hand.

The doors at the end of the hall are already open and the bed's about to disappear. I want to run after them. Beg them, "Please, don't take my daddy."

Even if I ran now, I couldn't catch up.

I know they're taking him somewhere to get help, but there's something I need him to know.

The gurney's half-outside now and I yell the words as loud as I can, "Love you, Dad!"

It comes out hollow. Flat. I can picture the letters of each word materializing from my mouth and shattering on the floor. The doors close, slowly, mechanically, just like my words.

Everyone—nurses, doctors, bleeding E.R. patients—they're all looking at me.

"Isn't it a little late?" I imagine them saying. *"Shouldn't he know that by now?"*

I should have told him. Not in the casual brief way I did in telephone good-byes, but face-to-face and eye-to-eye. It'd be uncomfortable but only because it'd be real.

Under the harsh fluorescent lights and the smell of antiseptic, I regret saying the words. Not because they aren't true or because everyone is staring at me. I just don't want Dad to know I think he's dying.

Standing in the hallway, numbness begins replacing my artificial smile as a nurse approaches. "You know, you can go watch," she says.

We snap to life and hurry down the hall—walking, but quickly. We follow an invisible trail left by the stretcher—out the double-doors, under the red emergency sign, down a gray sidewalk. Our different paces form us into a procession, with me in the lead. I walk across black asphalt and reach the grass in front of the heli-pad.

How close can I be?

The crew is still strapping the stretcher in. I want to go over, stand at the door. Make sure everything's okay. But I stay on the grass, my sisters on each side.

"Dad, always wanted to take a helicopter ride," Jennifer says.

We smile. He really did.

Mom runs over and takes a few pictures of Dad. We take pictures of everything.

"Too bad Dad doesn't have a camera for the flight," Melissa says.

The whole crew and Dad are in now and the doors are shut. I'm expecting them to take off at any moment, but several minutes pass with nothing.

Two nurses also stand on the grass; a few feet separating loved ones from healers. One of them calls out, "It's about to get cold."

"What?"

"When the helicopter starts. It'll get really cold."

It's early spring in northern Utah. It's already cold. We're wearing coats. The blades begin to turn, shooting a breeze towards us. I turn to the nurse and smile. It is a bit chilly.

The blades turn faster and faster and when there's enough lift to raise the helicopter a couple feet into the air it's no longer just a breeze. It's like a thousand blow dryers pounding us with ice-cold air. My hair flies back and wind shakes my cheeks and flattens my face.

"You can see your breath," Jennifer yells.

My lips purse and blow a spiraling stream of whiteness. It smokes beneath my view of the helicopter, seeming to lift the chopper as the mist dissipates.

The helicopter flies up and then forward. I walk through the parking lot, eyes locked on the chopper, trying to follow it as long as I can. A small dot, it disappears behind trees and buildings. And then its drone fades completely away. With my head lifted, my eyes remain fixed on the nothingness in the sky where I'd last seen my father.

For us left behind, there's a moment of confusion. No one's told us what to do. We gather on the asphalt amongst parked cars, looking to each other to provide us with direction.

Mom finally breaks the silence. "I'm sorry there won't be Sunday dinner." And I know she's not talking about today. Someday, there won't be Sunday dinner. I put my arm around her. She smiles and a tear rolls down her cheek.

"It's an hour drive to McKay-Dee," Jennifer announces. "I'll take Mom. Melissa, go to the house and pack a bag for them."

"What about me?" I ask.

Jennifer looks at me. "You've got Hudson to take care of. Just go home. We'll take care of Dad."

Then, we bow our heads and my husband says a quick prayer. With plans in place, we break up to walk to our individual vehicles.

"Amanda, wait," Mom calls out.

It's just the two of us now, standing eye-to-eye in the parking lot. From under her arm, she pulls out a newspaper. She must have been holding it the whole time. It's still rolled and bound with a rubber band, and she holds it out to me like a diploma.

"Your paper?"

"You were upset."

I stare at the gray bundle for a moment. She's right. I'd been upset. About the paper. About slow cashiers, needed repairs, bad weather, not enough sleep.

I had been upset.

I take the newspaper from her hands. Smile. Say goodbye.

Back home, I sit on our couch and peel off the elastic. The outside air has soaked into the pages, making them cool and crisp. The smell of both the rubber band and the recycled paper intensify in the warmth of the house. I separate the sections, arranging them on my coffee table. I leaf through every page. Scan the words and pictures. But I can't read a thing.

Not even the Sunday funnies.

IN THE SHIMMERING

I saw her in a shimmering
line of light, between
the sound waves
of steel guitar,
between the swirl
and shuffle
of high-flown skirts
and low-tipped Stetsons.

There she was,
the shadow
in a green dress.
The dream before
I heard her voice
and time began.

⌐Isaac Timm

BUMP IN THE NIGHT

Tim Keller

THE GYM WAS DARK. The dance committee always made sure the lights were low and the strobes intense. That way they could sneak out to drink, or make out behind the bleachers.

Music blared through speakers around the mezzanine where Janet Jaconet perched to watch. The slow song was over, replaced by some techno re-mix. The room throbbed with energy. One did not hear music like this, one felt it. Like a pagan festival, it was. Sweaty couples untangled themselves, jumping, gyrating, and slamming into one another. Some surfed the crowd, passing hand-to-outstretched-hand across the room. A few just held each other, swaying. Jan could always tell who was really in love. They were the ones who slow-danced even when the music got fast.

"What's the matter Jan?" Clare Jensen asked, breaking her concentration. "You've been pouting over here all night."

"Just waiting for a good song."

"Waiting for someone to ask, you mean," she cackled and skipped away.

God, I hate her, Jan thought. Especially because Clare was right. Jan was waiting. Well, hoping. No, praying would be more like it.

Then she saw—him. There, on the dance floor, the most beautiful boy she'd ever seen. His eyes closed, swaying, blissfully unaware that Clare was closing in.

Get away! Jan screamed in her mind. *She's a skank! Can't you see she's a skank?*

Jan watched helplessly as Clare danced closer.

Stalking her prey.

Clare's motions were stiff and disjointed by comparison, not really in time with the music. He, on the other hand, he was the music.

The song changed and in the confusion, Jan lost sight of them. She was immediately seized by a profound sense of loss.

Don't be an idiot, she thought. *Sure, he's cute, but, he's just another boy. The place is thick with them.* This didn't stop Jan from scanning the crowd. She caught a glimpse of Clare's sanguine gown as the back door slid shut.

It wasn't fair that a person like Clare should so easily meet a guy like that. He was way too good for her. She'd probably just sleep with him and then tell her Neanderthal boyfriend about it so he'd beat the poor guy up.

Not this time, Jan vowed and set off after them. But before Jan even reached the door, Clare was back—alone! She didn't look happy about it, either.

Could it be? The mighty Clare shot down? This guy was either a genius or gay, and she had to know which. Jan burst into the crisp autumn night, lifted her gown, and raced to catch him.

The boy was a hundred yards or so ahead when she spotted him, walking across the football field between the school and the highway. She saw him more clearly as he neared the glow of the streetlights. Jan could just make out his friendly call to a dog at the far end, but a single ear-splitting yelp brought her up short. She watched in shock as he caught the dog by the neck and threw it into the ground. Shock gave way to amazement when he ripped open the dog's throat and fed. He completely drained the animal, threw it into the path of an on coming car, and was gone.

Since that night, she'd watched him; studied his every move and with each night became more and more enraptured. Jan knew exactly what he was. His grace, impossibly perfect features, and innate sense of style—not to mention the occasional dead dog—gave him away. She'd never imagined she'd come across the creature that haunted her fantasies—a vampire, a real, live vampire.

Homecoming found Jan sitting in the same gym, watching the same people do and say the same things.

Nothing ever changes, she thought. Again she marveled at the stark contrast between her boy and the others in the room. Like a different species he was. *But of course,* she mused, *that's exactly what he is.*

Jan ached to be with him, to be a part of him. She downed the contents of her smuggled flask.

Courage in a bottle, she thought, making her way to him.

"Umm, hi," she muttered. "I'm—"

"Janet," he finished for her.

His voice gave her chills, his eyes so deep she could lose herself in them.

"I asked around," he offered smiling warmly. "I'm Jason."

Janet stared at her shoes. She wasn't used to being this forward and, to her horror, couldn't think of anything to say.

Jason laughed and put his arm around her shoulder. "It's such a beautiful evening; would you care to take a walk with me?"

She nearly fainted from excitement as he led her along the same route as the first time she'd seen him. Arm in arm, they crossed the field and into a stand of trees. For the first time in a long time, Jan was happy. Gradually, she found her voice again.

"This is nice," she gushed.

"Shh," he whispered. "Let's not spoil this by talking." His lips brushed her cheek, his hands, so soft, so gentle, yet unimaginably strong; it was everything she'd imagined and more. He laid her down, tugging at her clothes, almost ripping them off.

She reveled in his body, taut muscles under smooth, silky skin; the intensity of emotion so powerful she could scarcely breathe as he brought her to climax.

"I love you," she gasped.

Jason collapsed on top of her.

"I know what you are," she whispered, "and I love you."

Jason raised his head and peered at her quizzically.

"I know what you are," she repeated. "I know and I don't care. I've been watching you. I love you and I want to be with you forever."

"Forever?"

"Yes."

"And you—you really know what I am?"

"Oh, yes."

"No more pretending, then." Jason pulled her gently to her feet and hurled her into a tree.

Agony erupted in her head, then nothing.

The world came slowly into focus, and she found herself hanging by her hands—somewhere.

"You needn't bother screaming," he said. "No one will think to look for you here."

"Jason?"

"The one and only," he quipped.

"What—why?" she rasped.

"Why? It's what I do, that's why."

"But the animals, Clare, we made love, I thought—"

"I have needs!" He laughed, wiping the blood from her face, then licking his finger. "Hmm, besides," he said, "it sweetens the meat. Oh, the animals—a sad necessity of the modern age, I'm afraid. It's the same with Clare. A girl like her goes missing and the whole world goes nuts. An emo chick like you? No offense, but nobody gives it a second thought."

"You—you don't have to do this," she said, looking desperately for a way out.

Maybe, she thought. *Maybe someone will come.* "I won't tell anyone, I swear."

Jason looked casually through her belongings, her clothing, her jewelry, her purse and, finally, her phone. He laughed, stopping at one of her pictures. Jason held it up for her to see a picture of her and her younger brother. The phone bathed their faces in its cold blue light.

"Like lambs to the slaughter," he said. "The world at your finger-tips,—your lives all but guaranteed. But that's not enough, is it? You run around so desperate to be something, anything else. Well, con-gratulations, little girl. You found what you were looking for, except, I'm not your savior. I'm the boogie man." He laughed. "The monster in your closet, I am what goes bump in the night."

"But I love you!" She sobbed.

"Sucks for you, sweetness," he said, dousing her belongings with lighter fluid. "I don't even know what that is. You're nothing but livestock to me."

He struck a match, watched it burn almost to his fingers, and then tossed it on the pile.

"An entrée," he said. "Sounds better in French, don't you think? More civilized?"

He crushed the phone in his hand, tossed it on the fire, and turned to face her once more.

"Oh, I see," he said. "You thought we'd be soul mates; that you'd save me from my miserable existence. Then we'd be the star-crossed lovers you dreamt of in your bed at night? Did you ever stop to think what that would mean? No? No matter."

She shrieked as he sank his teeth into her breast and sucked long and deep. He stopped to lap at a rivulet of blood escaping down her flat stomach.

Jan's heart slowed as she watched the flames burn down.

"Mmm," Jason frowned. "Not as sweet as before," he said. "Listen, if you could manage to control your fear, just a little, I'd appreciate it."

She managed only a low moan.

"There's no point," he reasoned. "After all, fear is for people that have a chance. If you could just accept the inevitable, please? If you loved me as much as you say—no? Oh well. Spicy it is."

MATRIMONIALE
(Cerchiara de Calabria, Italy)

Lights of hillside village
wink and glow like jewels,
these two of glossy hair,
deep brown eyes, tender smiles.

Day dawns. Women dress bride;
her image smiles, reflects in Cheval
mirror. Satin chemise, silk under-slip,
yards of organdy, lace, glide over bride's
head, shimmer in a pool at her feet.

Groom enters, smiles, places
proprietary kiss—back of her neck.
Photographer's camera continues
winking its shuttered eye.

Wedding procession winds over
centuries-old cobblestones. Villagers
wave, call greetings. Chiesa de San Piedro
awaits in Baroque splendor. Clock-tower
bells announces wedding, ring out
in throaty brass tones—bell soup.

Bride cuts ribbon draped over church
portal. Gardens of flowers decorate pews.
A walk down aisle, hands clasped—
moment of reflection—wonder—joy.

Village priest, mitered hat, white
cape, stands at altar. Circlets of flowers
placed above heads as priest chants.
Rings exchanged, holy vows given
pronouncing them husband and wife.

Let the festa begin! Porchetta, panini,
biscotti, manicotti, ravioli, baskets
passed over heads to eager hands.
Carafes of garnet vino, filled, refilled.

Grandpapa bursts into scratchy song,
"Bella Mia". Guests laugh, clap, join in.

Va Bene!

Wedding dance begins. Random notes
pinned on bridal gown as they twirl on
confetti-draped floor, money-covered
at dance's-end. Groom gently removes
lire notes, places into bow-covered
Basket-a welcome nest of white.

Time passes, unnoticed. Music, dancing,
greetings. Wedding cake, flower frosted.
passed hand-to-hand. Champagne toasts,
glasses raised. "Salud", "Chi-Chi!".
Favors given: small crystal bells in
cotton beds. Attendants gather, giggle.
Bouquet tossed, portending next bride.

Bride and Groom depart amid boisterous
commotion. Dark night skies sparkle with
constellations, write love stories in sky.
A necklace of days ahead: a new life begins.

Irene Hastings

BRING THE JACKETS

Chadd VanZanten

I'M STILL IN MY NIGHTGOWN, but Terry's got the car almost packed. I sit in the kitchen and watch him through the window, trying to figure it out. He's made about twenty trips so far. Sometimes he takes just one thing with him. Like just the water jug. Other times he takes a big armload of stuff and drops it on the driveway as he goes. A couple times he goes out and brings something back into the house.

He props open the door with Mazy's Big Wheel, then trips over it as he comes back in. On the next trip out, he's got the big red ice chest with my beachbag on top.

He stops at the kitchen and says, "Babe, want me to grab you a jacket?"

I wish. A couple hours of rain would be a perfect excuse to stay home, but the sky is an ugly, spotless blue.

"What makes you think we're gonna need jackets?"

"Supposed to be windy and cold up there later. Internet even said so."

It's eight in the morning and he's sweating already. His glasses slide down to the tip of his nose. He wiggles his face to keep them from falling off.

"Not once in how many years have we needed jackets."

"So, want me to bring 'em?"

"Sure, bring the jackets, babe. Bring your mittens while you're at it."

He goes on out and throws his weight behind the cooler to cram it into the hatchback, but he bangs his head on the edge of the car. The beachbag falls, and my books and sunglasses spill out. Terry rubs his head, then bends down to pick up my things. His asscrack

129

emerges into the perfect sunlight.

Usually, it's me prodding him to get ready. Which is fine. If anyone has a right to hate my family's big camping trip, it's Terry. He's the one my brothers will de-pants or shove off the pier.

My dad won't do anything about it. Last year I said, "Daddy, you gotta do something about Derek. Tell him to lay off Terry."

He said, "Ah, Shelly, that'd just be blood in the water."

I'm not sure how things got turned around, but Terry comes in and says, "All packed."

He's so sweaty he has to change his t-shirt, jiggling as he pulls a fresh one over his belly. It's his favorite one—black, with a picture of some new military jet that costs a bazillion dollars.

"When're you gonna get ready?" he puffs, combing down his hair with his hand.

"What if we didn't go?" I ask. "We could stay here and grill some chicken."

He frowns. "You don't like it when I grill. You say it's never cooked all the way."

"We'll go out, then."

"Nah," he says, "your family'd kill us. You even said so. Why don't you wanna go?"

"I dunno. Derek and Bryan can be such jerks."

He waves his hand. "I just ignore 'em."

"Derek pushed you in the lake last year," I remind him. "You just about lost your inhaler."

"No, that was two years ago. Last year he put ambrosia in my sleeping bag. Way down inside."

"That's what I mean. They're such jerks."

He shakes his head. "You're gonna wanna talk to your mom. Mazy's been dying to see the cousins. C'mon, we gotta get moving if we want a good spot."

He goes down the hall and calls Mazy. I get in the shower.

When I was a kid, I couldn't wait to go to the lake. It's where I learned to swim, where I first kissed a boy. July fourth weekend, we'd play so hard we'd be asleep in the back of my Uncle Ricky's truck well before first the fireworks exploded out over the lake.

I sit on the bed with my wet hair, thinking of things we could do if we didn't go—nap in the backyard, read. Mazy would run in the sprinkler, her panties wet and sagging. We'd light sparklers.

Terry gives the horn a couple quick toots to keep me moving. I put on a sleeveless collared shirt that makes me look a little less chubby. When I come out, Terry opens the door for me, and I slump into the car. Mazy's already strapped into her car seat.

I put on my seatbelt and watch Terry hustle around to the driver's side. He gets in and we back onto the street.

"Buckle you, Daddy," Mazy says.

He puts on his seatbelt one-handed as we take a corner, and we just about sideswipe Mrs. Shultz in her Oldsmobile.

"Slow down, babe, jeeze," I say.

"Yeah, Daddy, jeeze," says Mazy.

Terry eases up, but it seems like he's leaning forward, like it'll make us go faster. I watch him as we pass by the houses and cul de sacs. He's grinning a little, but with the same expression he gets when he finally decides to jump off the high-dive at the city pool.

"What?" I ask him. "What is with you."

He shrugs. "I'm just excited."

We drive through town and get on the frontage road. He's definitely leaning forward, definitely grinning.

"Have you got some sort of plan?" I ask. "Are you gonna to try to pull something on my brothers?"

Terry looks at the speedometer for no reason.

"You can't beat them, Terry. Derek'll see you coming from a mile away."

He glances over, shows me the grin.

"Oh, you are planning something. This is so not-a-good idea."

He says, "I just want to get there, okay? We gotta get a good spot this year."

That's true. Dad always reserves a huge camping area, but if we're late we'll have to camp by the water with the mosquitoes, or on the hillside where everything's slanted.

I quiz Terry about what he packed.

"Did you get bugspray?"

"Yes."

"Sunblock?"

He hands me his phone. "Here. Open the first checklist."

I scroll through it. It's everything I'd pack, plus a few things I'd forget, like the marshmallow sticks. It's a good list, and I'm getting ready to say so when I see the last item.

Kite.

I look up from the phone. "Kite? You brought the kite?"

He looks at the speedometer.

This is not a regular kite like from the supermarket. It's a special stunt kite, and Terry put it on our credit card without telling me. This was five or six years ago, before Terry started working at Barr-Kane. The kite cost a lot of money, and we didn't have a lot of money.

I knew why he wanted it. Not very many people get to be exactly what they want to be in life, and that's too bad. But some people want to be the one thing they can never be, and that's Terry. He somehow got it in his head that he should be a fighter pilot. He loves jets, knows everything about them, but he's got so many health issues he never had a prayer of going into the military, let alone getting close to any jets.

His mom once told me, "The Air Force recruiter wouldn't even give him a free t-shirt."

Terry's great at what he does, he's great with computers, but get him close to any airplane and he gets a look in his eyes, like a kid seeing the only Christmas present he wants, knowing he'll never get it. I can't go to the air shows with him. He goes alone.

I let him keep the kite. Grudgingly.

The lake would be a great place to fly it, too, but Terry knows I don't like to even look at the kite, and it's one of the things we still fight about. He has to go to a park on the other side of town to fly it. He's in a kite club with his buddies and they all fly their kites together—without wives. They buy things for their kites, pamper them. The wallpaper on Terry's laptop is him holding his kite. We have a baby—a human-being daughter—and he sets his wallpaper to a kite picture.

"So, you're going to be off flying your kite the whole time," I say.

"No. Not the whole time."

"I hate that kite."

"You've never even seen me fly. I'm one of the best in the club now. Josh even said so."

As if bringing that prick into this is going to help. Josh, el presidente of the kite boy club.

"Mazy's excited to see me fly. Right, sweetie?"

Mazy hides her face with her arm and says, "I'm not diposta say anything about it if Mommy's around."

"Mommy knows about it now," I tell her. And that's when I get it—his favorite t-shirt, packing up the car, his diving-board grin.

"Is this your plan? The kite is your plan?"

He stops grinning.

"Oh, Terry. How is a kite your plan?"

He clams up, but he speeds the rest of the way, so we're nice and early. The camping area is a grassy half-acre next to a cove on the north end of the lake. Along one side stands a wall of big cottonwoods that shimmer and hiss in the lightest breeze. On the other side, grassy hills that glow at sunset. Down at the shore between the willow trees there's a gravelly beach.

Derek hasn't shown up yet, so the space next to my dad's camp trailer is open. Terry gets our tent out of the car.

"You think Derek'll be mad if we set up right next to you?" I ask my dad.

"He'll get over it. He knows to get here early."

Terry and I put up the tent without talking much. Terry's sweating again, pulling up his drooping shorts. The sun climbs and more people show up. Pretty soon Mazy is swept away in a swarm of cousins. They go to the water and throw rocks, the same rocks I threw when I was little—rounded and smooth, like globs of semisolid earth that somehow hardened. The water is so calm the rings expand way out into the lake, like they could spread to the other side.

"Wonder where Derek is," says Terry.

My parents shrug in unison. In their matching deluxe camping chairs, they both sit the same way—slumped down, right leg crossed over left, arms draped on the armrests. King and queen of the campground. I unfold a chair next to them and Terry sits on the ground. He pulls up handfuls of grass and throws it in the air to check for wind, but it falls straight down.

It's lunchtime before Derek pulls into the campground in his enormous Chevy. It glitters with so much chrome, Mom and Dad shade their eyes even though they're both wearing sunglasses. We hear the music thumping all the way across the campground. Behind the truck is a trailer with two jet-skis.

"What an outfit," says Dad, shaking his head.

"Hurts my eyes," says Mom.

The cousins hoard around as Derek dismounts the truck, even though they know it will probably be tomorrow before he gives out any rides on his jet-skis. Derek towers above even the tallest of them, wider than any two. He looks the place over as if he just conquered it.

Brooke hops out of the other side. Her huge sunglasses hide everything but the tip of her nose and her mouth and some of her forehead.

Then Bryan swings in. His truck is smaller than Derek's but just as loud and shiny. He gets out. Derek grabs him and they wrestle. The kids back away. It's like watching two buffalo contend for territory. Pretty soon Bryan's in a chokehold. His face turns purple before Derek lets him go.

Brittney gets out of Bryan's truck and finds her place next to Brooke. They mince through the grass in their high-heeled sandals like they're afraid they'll step in something.

"Stevie," Brooke warns one of the little cousins, "keep those muddy paws offa me."

The two wives have the same big sunglasses, the same crisp, pale clothes. Brittney's skinny, but not as skinny as Brooke. No one can be as skinny as Brooke. They come over and give Mom and Dad hugs without really touching them.

"How you guys doing?" asks Brooke. "We've been meaning to come over. How're you getting around?"

Mom and Dad look at each other.

"Getting around what?" says Dad.

Brittney stands with her arms tightly folded. She keeps adjusting the way her bangs lay across her forehead, as if it's the one thing she can do without permission from Brooke.

Brooke touches Mom's arm and says, "Tell me you brought your fried chicken."

"Sure," says Mom. "Want a piece?"

"Oh, no," she says. She pats her flat, featureless tummy, as though that explains her answer. "But I have got to get that recipe."

I can't help myself. I say, "Brooke, you can cook?"

Mom shoots me a look. Brooke fakes a laugh. Dad laughs for real.

"Shelly," coos Brooke. She tip-toes over to me. "Lookit you, girl. I can see why you always wear that shirt." She leans in for the no-touch hug and says, "It really slims you down."

Derek and Bryan set up a couple campchairs in the shade, and the two wives go and sit and thumb their phones. Then Derek comes toward us with his tent. It's a six-man cabin tent, but it's tucked under his arm like a newspaper. When I was a kid, I loved all my brothers and sisters, but Derek was my favorite—I thought he was a happy, bighearted kid. When I left home for school, I thought I'd sort of lose track of him, but instead I got to know him a lot better. I could finally see him the way other people did, and I understood why some people never liked him. Or were afraid of him.

Derek looks at Dad's camper, then our tent, then Terry.

Terry's frozen, not even blinking. I half expect him to change colors to better blend in with his surroundings. Derek throws down his tent and I feel the impact of it in the ground.

"Terry, why'd you stick your tent right here?"

Dad says, "Well, Son, it's known as camping."

Derek snorts. "But if he'd move ten feet over, me and Bry could put our tents in here. He's hogging all the room."

"We got the whole campground," says Dad. "How much room do you need?"

Derek snorts again and keeps glaring at Terry. Terry looks down and I should be embarrassed for him, but I don't want to think about what would happen if he tried to stand up to Derek.

"Nobody needs to be moving already-put-up tents in this heat," says Dad. He points across the campground. "There's some nice spots by Ricky's firepit."

"I don't wanna sleep by Ricky. He snores."

Mom pipes up. "So do you, sweetie."

"The queen has spoken," says Dad.

"Fine," says Derek. He scoops up the tent. "Damn waste of space, though."

"Language," says Mom.

"We're camping over there," Derek yells at Bryan. "Too crowded over here."

"See that, Shelly?" says Dad. "Blood in the water."

"Why's he like that," I ask.

Dad takes his time answering. "Hard to say. I honestly don't think he wants to be like that. Sometimes I think he's just waiting for the world to tell him to knock it off."

Derek opens a beer and recruits some kids to set up his tent. He heckles and trips them while they work. Bryan sets up his own tent and Derek heckles him, too.

When they finish, they throw off their shirts and back the trailer down the gravelly beach. The jet-skis float free and they climb on. Kids crowd along the shore to watch. Bryan turns for open water, but Derek races right at the kids. When he's twenty feet out, he steers hard left and sprays them all with a big sheet of water. Then he's gone, too. The kids stand dripping as the sound of the machines fade.

Terry heads straight for the car and he's back in one minute with his kite bag. It's got special pockets for all the controls and spools. He lays it out and then looks over at the kids, but they're still down at the shoreline.

He kneels down and works on the kite like he's reviving some huge, sleepy bat. It's almost as wide as he is tall.

"What's he got over there?" says Dad.

I sigh. "It's his kite."

"Looks like a hang glider."

A few kids spot Terry and begin watching him from a distance. He positions the kite and trails the strings across the grass. Stevie and a few other kids wander over. Some are damp and muddy. Some are already sunburned.

"But there's no wind," says Mom.

136

"It's a special kite." I tell her. "It doesn't need wind."

Terry warns the kids to stand back. He says, "Please don't step on the lines, okay you guys?"

Stevie stamps on them and then runs off. The rest stick around, asking questions.

When everything's ready, Terry puts his headphones in and takes up the paddles. They're like marionette paddles, but styled like the controls of a jet. He stands there a moment with his head down, like what he will do next is important. Then, in step to the music we can't hear, he pulls the controls and shuffles backwards. His belly jiggles like mad, but his movements are weirdly graceful.

The kite lifts fifty feet into the air and the kids cheer.

Dad flips up his sunglasses and says, "Would you look at that."

Terry yanks on one handle and the kite peels off to one side. The kids run following with upturned faces and arms reaching skyward.

A cool breeze starts up, as if conjured by Terry's cryptic circling. Wind shadows ripple and swerve out on the lake. The sweat on my neck turns chilly.

The cottonwood leaves begin to seethe and the kite makes a flapping sound. Terry puts on a show for us. The kite soars, stalls, then plunges down, almost hitting the ground before turning up again. The kids chase it.

Terry looks over his shoulder at me. Through his glasses I see his eyes blaze deliriously. I wave at him and he tilts back his head and laughs.

This goes on for over an hour. I sit catching up with Mom and Dad, but we pause to clap for the good tricks. Everyone's watching now. The kids have their chairs set up like an audience. Even Brooke and Brittney look up from their phones from time to time.

Mom says, "I like it when it almost crashes but he saves it at the last second."

"I like the figure-eight," says Dad.

Something is happening out over the lake. Wet air colliding with hot air or cool air colliding with dry. Terry could explain it right, but the result is a line of clouds, with grey underneath, forming on the south side of the lake. The breeze picks up and waves march into shore.

My dad flips up his sunglasses and scans the water. "Those boys ought to be getting back. Looks choppy out there."

The wind grows strong enough to send the kite into endless cork-screws. Terry's face is red and he's breathing hard. Just when we think he's out of tricks, he leaps over the kite strings and works the handles behind his back. Uncle Ricky laughs and shakes his head.

Only Dad and I notice when Derek and Bryan bounce over the waves and glide back into shore. No kids mob them, no one asks for a ride.

They beach the jet-skis and dry off. Then they come up from the water talking loud, but everyone's watching the kite. Terry brings it low for the kids to pet it. It hovers nearly motionless a few feet off the ground. The kids touch it and jerk their hands back, like it's a living thing, and then they run away squealing.

Derek and Bryan stand a ways off, pointing and smirking. As if planning what to do about it. After awhile they get out a football and try to draft Uncle Ricky and others into a game, but no one wants to play.

Dad points at the kite and says, "Oh, didja see that one?" but I catch him sneaking glances at the boys. They're tossing the ball to each other, but they're watching Terry.

Then Derek motions for Bryan to go long, and Bryan takes off running. He jumps over the kids in their seats, and when he's under the kite, Derek launches the ball. It looks like he's too far away to hit the kite, but the wind carries the throw beyond even Derek's range, and we gasp as the ball smacks into the kite like a missile.

The kite veers over, collapsing. Something in it has come apart or snapped. It dives noisily into the grass and flutters there like a wounded pterodactyl.

Terry whips around to see where the ball came from. Everyone does. All eyes go to Derek. He stands there grinning, arms folded across his chest. Groans rise in a chorus above the wind.

"What," he shouts. "It was an accident."

"Daddy," I hiss, "will you do something?"

Dad holds up his hand and keeps watching.

Terry yanks out his headphones. His hair blows around. He kneels at the crash site and examines the great, injured bird. The kids circle in, heads bowed.

"Is she broken?" says Mazy.

"Nah," says Terry. "She's just fine."

When the kite rushes up the wind again, the whole campground roars. It loops up and up. The kids hoot. Derek sets his hands on his hips and spits in the grass.

Then the kite turns and begins to cross the campground. I look down at Terry. He's on the move, and when he stops, the kite is parked twenty feet above Derek's head like a UFO or the world's blackest raincloud. Derek sneers and steps to one side. The kite follows. Everyone laughs.

My heart sinks a little. It occurs to me that I was probably never too concerned about Derek humiliating Terry. It was always the opposite prospect that seemed worse.

Terry tightens his grip on the handles and makes a move like kung fu. The kite rips down from the sky and Derek flees stumbling through the grass. The nylon kite skin crackles like a machinegun as the kite streaks past. Derek staggers away but the kite takes after him.

Derek somehow comes up with the football and flings it at the kite. He manages a glancing blow, but the kite stays up. Derek dodges the kite, gets the ball, throws again. The battle goes on until they're at the water.

Mom and Dad stand up head to the shore. We all do.

"Bring it down," barks Derek. He's panting and he's got grass stuck to his face. He seats the football in his big hand and says, "Give me a clean shot."

Terry's got his back to the water. He lowers the kite so that it hovers in front of Derek, rattling like crazy. Derek fakes a throw. The kite doesn't move. He fires the ball and Terry rears back. The kite leaps clear and the ball spirals out over the lake. It splashes down and bobs in the water.

Everybody cheers. The kids are hopping and clapping. They crowd around Terry. Uncle Ricky runs over to pat him on the back.

Dad turns to me. "See that, Shelly?"

Derek stands with his back to us, watching his football. It has found some current in the lake that runs counter to the wind and it edges away into the open expanse of water, as if it had only been waiting for an opening to strike out alone.

Terry shows Uncle Ricky how to work the kite and then hands over the controls. Uncle Ricky tugs on the paddles, and the kite wobbles through a few turns.

"Would you look at that," laughs Uncle Ricky.

Mazy climbs into Terry's arms and reaches into the air after the kite.

"Oh, she's freezing," says Terry.

Mom says, "I've got some jackets in the trailer."

"That's okay," I say. I slip an arm around Terry's waist. "We've got some over in the car."

www.ingramcontent.com/pod-product-compliance
Lightning Source LLC
Chambersburg PA
CBHW071348170626
46811CB00003B/1039